PREACHING

Preaching in Stories

James A. Feehan

THE MERCIER PRESS
and distributed in Britain by
FOWLER WRIGHT BOOKS

The Mercier Press Limited
4 Bridge Street, Cork
24 Lower Abbey Street, Dublin 1

Fowler Wright Books Limited
Burgess Street, Leominster
Herefordshire, England

British Library Cataloguing in Publication Data
Feehan, James
    Preaching in stories.
    1. Christian church. Preaching.
    I. Title
    251

THE MERCIER PRESS
ISBN 0-85342-887-5

FOWLER WRIGHT BOOKS
ISBN 0 85244 159 2

Acknowledgements

The author and publisher would like to thank the following authors, publishers and copyright holders for their permission to quote material for which they hold the copyright.

Fr Jack McArdle and Columba Press for material from It's Really Very Simple – Uncomplicating the Message; the Far East for permission to use the story by Fr Patrick Reilly; the Bible Societies for quotations from the Goods News Bible, published by the Bible Societies and Collins © American Bible Society 1976, used by permission.

Every effort has been made to trace the owners of copyright material and it is hoped that no copyright has been infringed. If we have inadvertently infringed any copyright we apologise and will make the necessary correction at the first opportunity.

Printed by Litho Press Co., Midleton, Co. Cork.

Contents

TO THE MEMORY
OF
MY PARENTS
ELLEN & THOMAS FEEHAN
WHO TOLD ME MY FIRST STORIES

Introduction

This book was compiled for a special purpose, and if it should not satisfy those for whom it was intended, no preface can save it.
ROBERT BRIDGES (1844-1930)

The story is told of an English bishop who invariably began his talks like this, 'Of course I really don't know why you people should be listening to me, at all.' It would have been a fitting apologia for what follows but the trouble with the bishop was that people took him at his word and stopped listening. If you, dear reader, have not stopped reading or are about to return this book to the shelf bear with me while I tell you why I had the effrontery to write it. It was motivated by a number of convictions gleaned from almost four decades of preaching.

Firstly, the Church of God across the world needs preachers. 'Jesus went... and preached,' Mark tells us (1:14) and he calls upon those who have heard his word to speak it to others. He has chosen to pass on his message through people.

Secondly, in a television age with an educated congregation the challenge to the preacher is formidable. Anyone can preach a good homily once, to do so Sunday after Sunday is the problem.

Thirdly, there is widespread boredom in the pews today. Preaching, it is claimed, has had its day. It is out. So often it's so dull, sleepy and unrelated to the everyday lives of contemporary Christians that people are beginning to vote with their feet as well as their concentration.

Fourthly, with the communications revolution we have passed from a word culture to a picture culture. This demands creativity from the preacher if he is to get his message across to the pews. The story of God must be linked to his own story of faith and the life experience of his listeners.

Finally, the new emphasis on narrative as distinct from systematic theology calls for a re-appraisal of the storytelling process in preaching the word on Sundays. After all, our faith began with storytelling. Jesus was a master storyteller. He taught and preached in pictures. 'He would not speak to them without using parables' (Mk 4:34).

In the period of oral tradition before the Gospels were written down his stories were told and re-told. The format of the early Christian assembly was to gather the people, tell the stories and break the bread. When the first Gospel came to be written its most striking characteristic was its vivid storytelling. Mark was a born storyteller who filled his pages with unforgettable pictures. So, the storytellers were there before the theologians. Theology really began as a reflection on story and in the course of time creeds, dogmas and catechisms were superimposed on the storytelling process. In these our own times there is a notable revival in storytelling, a shift from the dogmas and creeds which dominated our thought patterns in the past to what is now called narrative theology.

For those of us ordained in the1950s and early 1960s all is changed, changed utterly. Some of us can still rattle off the catechism answer telling us that the three chief parts of the Mass were the Offertory, Consecration and Communion. We were taught in the seminary that it was at most a venial sin to miss the scriptural readings and the sermon. In fact you were still in time for Mass up to when the priest removed the veil from the chalice. Then came the Second Vatican Council and its first document *The Constitution on the Sacred Liturgy*.

The essential parts of the Mass were now two: the Liturgy of the Word and the Liturgy of the Eucharist. The sermon became the homily and the vital link between the Word and the Eucharist. Not only did the Second Vatican Council declare the centrality of preaching but it called for a new style of preaching. The homily should proclaim, re-present and make effectively present 'God's wonderful works in the history of salvation'. And where were these 'wonderful works' to be found? In the Scriptures. The sermon was gone and we were back to the old liturgical homily of the early Church which proclaimed that God had acted and continues to act in our lives.

A short time ago I was given the rather unique gift of a Protestant church. Because of a dwindling congregation the Church of Ireland authorities in a magnanimous gesture handed the building over to the Catholic community. The most striking feature of the church was the prominence given to the word of God. Out in front facing the congregation were a huge oak-carved pulpit and lectern; the altar was a small communion table relatively hidden in the background. With powerful visual stimuli such as these the centrality of preaching in Protestant worship was not lost on the new congregation.

Despite the promise of the Second Vatican Council and the winds of change that accompanied it the modern preacher finds himself facing a congregation which seems either unable or unwilling to listen. Prophets of doom are confidently predicting that the days of preaching are over; that it is an outmoded form of communication in a television age; that people are incapable of sustained listening for more that five or six minutes and that if you cannot actually hear the switch-off you can see it in the glazed looks in the pews.

This growing dissatisfaction with the quality of preaching is reflected in some of the surveys carried out on the subject. The most recent of these, *To Proclaim His Word* a report prepared for the Irish Liturgical Commission, presenting detailed surveys carried out amongst clergy, adult laity and students concerning their attitudes to and evaluation of the current celebration of the Liturgy of the Word reveals a high level of dissatisfaction with the prevailing standard of preaching. A few years ago the American Bishops published *Fulfilled in Your Hearing* in response to numerous surveys indicating the questionable quality of preaching in Catholic churches. Only a few years ago *Time* Magazine carried a feature on the decline of American preaching and Mary Kenny in a recent issue of *The Sower* asserts that one could travel the length and breadth of Ireland now and not hear a decent sermon in a month of Sundays, 'except of course,' she adds tongue-in-cheek 'should you stray into the robust ultra-Protestant bailiwick of such persons as the Rev. Ian Paisley who, whatever his politics, delivers a mighty sermon when the mood is on him.'

It is claimed that congregations are being subjected to a seemingly infinite variety of canned homilies. 'Some preachers,' writes Joseph Donders, 'give beautiful pieces of oratory. The listener is meant to be amazed by the learnedness and never-ending flow of words hardly ever heard before. Other preachers give sermons in which God is praised and thanked and glorified and implored. It does not become clear why all this is done. Other preachers use their sermons to explain what certain Bible texts mean. They often are more interested in what these texts might have meant to the Corinthians or Romans, than to the Baltimorians, the New Yorkers and the Californians.'

All very depressing, but there is an oasis of hope. It is provided by preachers who offer their people not just a skilled performance in the pulpit but a caring ministry; who help their flock to grow in grace through Jesus; who seek to build bridges between the Word and the world; who tell their own story of faith with humility, courage and sincerity and who, in telling it, relate the story of God to the stories of their listeners. Finally, I thank the long-suffering congregations of Thurles, Boherlahan and Dualla who have been the anvil on which I have forged the stories and reflections in this book. I express my special thanks to the Quinn family for their painstaking efforts in turning pages of illegible handwriting into a clean typescript.

JAMES A. FEEHAN

1

The Trouble with Preaching

Many leave the Church because the language flowing from the pulpit has no meaning for them; it has no connection with their own life and simply bypasses many threatening and unavoidable issues... The trouble with preaching is becoming even more troublesome.

KARL RAHNER

There are many prophets of doom in today's Church who are confidently predicting that the days of preaching are over. The ambo has replaced the pulpit, sermons have become sermonettes and the homily has become a sort of spiritual *hors d'oeuvre* before Holy Communion. Add to that the massive boredom in the pews, the people voting first with their concentration and then with their feet, and what can we say but, pity the poor preacher! It may be of some comfort to those of us who are concerned with the current disenchantment with preaching to recall that St Paul in one memorable sermon failed to hold the attention of Eutychus, a lapse of concentration that had disastrous consequences, and just listen to this scathing indictment of preachers from the pen of Anthony Trollope: 'There is perhaps, no greater hardship at present inflicted on mankind in civilised and free countries, than the necessity of listening to sermons. No one but a preaching clergyman has in these realms the power of compelling an audience to sit silent and be tormented. No one but a preaching clergyman can revel in platitudes, truisms and untruisms and yet receive as his undisputed privilege, the same respectful demeanour as though words of impassioned eloquence, or persuasive logic, fell from his lips... let a barrister attempt to talk without talking well, and he will talk but seldom. A Member of Parliament can be coughed down or counted out, Town Councillors can be tabooed but no one can rid himself of the preaching clergyman. He is the bore of the age... the nightmare that disturbs our Sunday rest, the incubus that loads our religion and makes God's service distasteful!'

Trollope's scorn was no doubt motivated by his dislike for 'the damp, sandy-haired, saucer-eyed, red fisted Obadiah Slope,' chaplain to the hen-pecked Bishop of Barchester. The time and the place may have changed but the play-actors remain the same and we have to ask ourselves why is it that preaching today manages to reduce to a state of boredom those Sunday worshippers whom it does not succeed in keeping away altogether?

Whenever Queen Victoria visited a town or village it was customary for the bells to be rung as a mark or respect. In one instance when this time honoured custom was not observed the Royal Chamberlain berated the Mayor for this affront to royalty. The embarrassed local official replied that he could give ten good reasons for not ringing the bells. 'The first,' he said, 'is that we haven't got any bells.'

'That will do,' snapped the royal official, 'you can forget about the other nine.'

If there is one basic reason for the glazed looks and the switch-off in the pews it must surely be the communications revolution. Television, tabloids and modern advertising have brought about an epochal change in people's listening habits. We have moved from a word culture to a picture culture and surveys have shown that people today are incapable of sustained listening for more than five or six minutes. Just look at the news bulletins. News and opinion are communicated by a quick paragraph from one voice

followed by a clip of film, or another quick paragraph from
another voice. News items are interspersed by interviews,
many of them aggressive especially to the speaker who
wants a platform for his own. Robin Day, Olivia O'Leary and
Phil Donahue have superseded the preachers of yesteryear.
These communicators do not deliver speeches and they see
to it that no one else does.

Where does all this leave the preacher? He has to deal with
a television conditioned congregation which can no longer
listen without looking. It is harder for people to listen atten-
tively and responsively and we can no longer assume that
they either want to listen or indeed are able to listen. We have
inherited our methods of communication from, as far as the
moderns are concerned, a now discredited past. We have, so
to speak, been left standing by the communications revolution.

It must be admitted however, that there have been
attempts to preach in the modern style. Homilies have become shorter and have been illuminated by apt and telling
illustrations; the old oratorical style and flamboyant gestures
have given way to an easy armchair approach. Some churches
have introduced twin pulpits in which two preachers debate
an issue or one interviews and quizzes the other. This has
proven popular at mid-week lunch-time meetings and at
mission time but might be out of place at Sunday worship
especially under the constraints of the six minute homily.

Audience participation has long been a feature of black
worship. They have had it in Africa for centuries and in
America the black worshipper not merely acknowledges the
word delivered by the preacher, he talks back. It is not
unusual to hear cries of 'Halleluiah!' 'Amen', 'tell it brother',
'sho' 'nough', 'yes sir.' The black person's 'Amen' means you
have said what I know to be true, although perhaps I could
not put it into your own words. You are speaking to me. You
are confessing my faith!

On one occasion, a zealot was continually interrupting the sermon and the preacher's patience finally evaporated and he said tartly, 'I would be grateful if the member of the congregation who keeps calling out "Praise The Lord" would kindly cease and remember that this is the House of God.' Of course we can be rather selective at times with our assent to the preacher's words. Take the case of Sharon. With fervent 'Amens' she apparently approved of everything the black preacher was saying in his sermon. To be sure, she did approve as long as he spoke of the love of God and the joy of being one of God's children but when he pointed an accusing finger at the congregation and spoke against gossip and tale-bearing Sharon's 'Amens' ceased and she said, 'There now he's done gone meddling; he has done gone and spoiled a good sermon.'

Once a black preacher whipped his congregation into a frenzy of enthusiasm with a sermon on Judgment Day. 'It says here is the Good Book,' he shouted, 'that there will be weeping and gnashing of teeth. Hear that you sinners... you shall weep and gnash your teeth.' One woman called out, 'Please Pastor Jones, ah ain't got no teeth'! To which the preacher determined that the Scriptures were going to be fulfilled thundered back, 'Mam... teeth will be provided!'

Another problem facing the preacher is the changing attitude to authority figures, the who-does-he-think-he-is syndrome. Anything which savours of establishment, Church, State, God, even the family, all the accepted authorities are being challenged. The preacher is traditionally an authority figure so he faces a growing resistance to authoritative pulpit announcements. During the abortion referendum campaign in Ireland the clergy were accused of abusing their powers when they preached on the biblical certainty of life and the rights of the unborn. A television debate on the use or abuse of the pulpit challenged the preacher's right to speak about poverty, social injustice, civil

rights, unemployment, crime, the environment, violence
and other issues which were filling the newspapers every
day. Stick to spiritual matters he was told. Others accused
priests for sitting on the fence and being silent on these
issues. This anti-authority mood cannot but affect the morale
of the preacher especially when he sees himself as a target for
the hostility of the young who more often than not vote with
their feet.

The preacher too has to face the sometimes unpalatable
fact that education is changing the people in the pews. There
was a time when the priest, the teacher, the doctor and the
occasional other professional person were the best educated
people at Sunday worship. It is not so now. The pews are now
filled with people whose knowledge and expertise are greater
than his especially when he strays from scriptural and theo-
logical paths. The changed situation has made the people
more questioning and critical. They are not prepared to
accept the drivel that is sometimes doled out to them nor will
they tolerate the use of the pulpit as a launching pad for the
bees that buzz in preachers' bonnets.

A young curate recently promoted to a more cultivated
parish went to an old priest seeking counsel. 'Father, I am
really frustrated in preaching to my new congregation. If I
speak on the effects of the pill there is an eminent gynaeco-
logist right in front of me; if I speak on English literature I am
cowed by the presence of a professor; if I instance something
from history, there is an historian ready to trip me up. What
shall I do?'

The old man replied, 'have you ever tried preaching the
Gospel to them? They probably know very little about that!'

History records a famous instance where a young Presby-
terian minister overawed by the presence of royalty in his
congregation reached his highest heights of oratory in this
prayer for Queen Victoria herself. 'Grant that as she grows to
be an old woman, she may be made a new man, and stand

before thee as a pure virgin, bringing forth sons and daughters to thy glory; and that in all peaceful causes she may go forth before her people like a he-goat on the mountains!' He wasn't asked to preach before royalty again!

Preachers still reeling from the culture shock of the 1960s and 1970s have now to face the fundamental problems of secularism and unbelief. They have to try and sow the seed of God's Word in people who live as though God did not exist and others who opt for an *à la carte* religion, expressing doubt and confusion regarding things like belief in angels, hell, purgatory and a whole range of moral teaching.

In a recent address to the National Conference of Priests of Ireland, Bishop Donal Murray of Dublin had this to say: 'Many people live in a world which has, for all practical purposes, no place for religion. Nobody ever prays in *Dynasty* or *Dallas!* Business tends to operate on the principle that generosity and compassion and social conscience are for suckers and are the path to bankruptcy. Religion, even for those who practise regularly and seriously, tends to be pushed into ever shrinking corners of life. In our own lives which are supposed to be centred on the Lord, is there not a growing secular content which is less than fully integrated into the spiritual?'

The secularism of a post-Christian age cannot but influence the morale of the preacher and indeed his mental and emotional approach to every phase of pastoral activity. One however should not despair of the power of the Word to move hearts apparently closed to the things of the Spirit. As Pope John Paul put it... 'it is impossible to eradicate completely the sense of God or to silence the conscience completely' (*Reconciliation and Penance*, 18).

The Vigil Mass introduced in 1983 presents a new and challenging problem particularly to preachers heretofore in the habit of reaching for pre-packed homily hints before, during or after Saturday night television. A priest may now find himself in the situation of having to preach at three liturgies on Saturdays: a funeral in the morning, a wedding in the afternoon and of course the evening Mass. He may find himself rushing away from a wedding reception with little or no preparation for the Vigil Mass. In a very perceptive feature on the Vigil Mass in *Intercom* (July/August 1988) Father Bernard Moloney has this to say: 'Every priest has heard the advice that he should begin preparing his weekend homily on the previous Monday and continue to chew over it during the week. This recommendation is now more urgent and cogent. The runway leading to the take off at the ambo has been considerably shortened. One fears that there are many "crashed on take-off" verdicts passed at Saturday suppers – which made no improvement on the "circled but couldn't land" verdicts passed heretofore at Sunday dinners!' Moloney then goes on to highlight another challenge to the preacher arising from the Vigil Mass – the number of people who come back for a Sunday Mass and within the space of sixteen hours have to sit through a repeat of the homily. This is a problem particularly in rural areas where priests are thinly spread. A situation like this makes it absolutely imperative that we put careful thought and preparation into what we have to say. Beginning on Monday, though highly commendable, has its problems for the priest caught up in the conflict between administration and mission. As well as the unpredictable demands of the pastoral ministry today's priest is expected to be a fundraiser, accountant, and school manager with its attendant calls to show expertise in plumbing and building. In the current scarcity of housekeepers he has to be on call to answer door bells and telephones as well as being proficient in the culinary skills and home economics. Caught up as he is in roles for which he has neither the time, the training nor the expertise can he be blamed if during the week he casts but a deferential nod in the direction of the Sunday homily?

The first priests in the early Church had a simple solution to these problems – they passed these chores over to lay people to whom they gave a sense of responsibility and importance by calling them deacons and note the reasons why they did this – it was so that they, the priests unencumbered by the burden of administration might give their 'full time to prayer and the work of preaching'(Acts 6:4).

Is there a message for us here?

2

The Trouble with Stories

The rarest and mightiest possession of the human Spirit can be discovered only by means of a story and by no other process of thinking.

GORDON CHALMERS

A famous Polish rabbi was once asked why the story had such persuasive power over people. 'How better to explain it,' he said 'than by means of a story: It happened once that Truth walked down the street of a village as naked as on the day he was born. "A streaker!" the people cried and ran into their houses, pulled the blinds and would have nothing to do with him. As Truth walked on alone wondering why he couldn't get across to people he saw Story approaching him. Story was decked out in fine clothes, gay colours and was a sight to see. "Why do you go around brooding, Truth?" he asked, "What is troubling you?"

'"Because nobody accepts me," responded Truth, "they run away from me whereas you are always invited into their houses. They love to sit around their fires listening to you. Why does every one avoid me?"

'"It's your nakedness," replied Story. "People today find it increasingly difficult to absorb naked truth. Use a little bit of imagination. I'll tell you what... I'll lend you some of my fine clothes and you just see how people will take to you."

'Truth followed this advice and decked himself out in Story's gay clothes. People no longer shunned him, they opened their doors to him and since that time Story and Truth have been inseparable companions, respected and loved by all.'

Stories like pictures are worth a thousand words. They provide powerful illustrative material in getting the message across but like all illustrations they have their limitations.

Some preachers use stories as attention grippers or ice-breakers to warm up the congregation. This is commendable provided the story is relevant to the message and does not dominate it. Often there is no connection between the story and what follows. We can be so carried away by the story that the story of God goes untold and the sheep are not fed. Secondly, a story should be told to highlight just one thing. This was Jesus' way of preaching in parables. He had just one point to get across and he did not need to explain the story for people to get the message. The preacher must resist the temptation of allegorical interpretation, that is pointing to numerous lessons to be learned from one story. Apart from the danger of the listeners becoming muddled or bored there is the time factor. Allegory in which every detail of the Bible story is made to represent a specific point has no part to play in the six minute homily. Augustine was a notorious offender in this respect. His allegorised interpretation of the Good Samaritan is well-known. The certain man is Adam; Jerusalem is the heavenly city; Jericho the moon (symbolising our mortality); the thieves are the devil and his angels. He sees the oil as hope; the wine as an exhortation to work; the beast as the flesh in which Christ came; the inn as the Church; the morrow as the Resurrection and the inn-keeper as the apostle Paul!

Another problem with stories is that they have a way of becoming dated, the more attractive ones tend to become hackneyed and in churches where the preachers change frequently we can never be sure that the same story has not been used the week before.

Even the Gospel stories and parables are not immune to this difficulty. They have been heard so often that they do not surprise anyone anymore. They have lost their bite and their sting. The trouble here is in the manner of presentation and interpretation. They are still historically time-bound, locked away in a first century Jewish straitjacket and over-laid by interpretations and explanations that are outdated and refer to insights and experiences from times that have vanished like the snows of yesteryear. Here is a clear case for creative preaching, for re-telling the old story in a fresh way to these people in this particular congregation in these new times. The creative preacher sees a relationship between the biblical story and the current event and is like the householder in the Gospel 'who takes new and old things out of his storeroom' (Mt. 13:52).

A good story speaks for itself and should never be restricted to one particular insight or interpretation. Stories say different things to different people. To read one story after another provides entertainment, to read one story slowly and reflectively can, according to Tony de Mello, produce mysticism. A good story should also stand on its own feet. The preacher should avoid attaching a moral to it or following it up with an explanation. Only rarely did Christ explain any of his parables and then only when he was asked later. A story is not the same as an illustration. The illustration needs to be explained, it points to something else. The story has its own reality and meaning. A good storyteller may sometimes conclude his homily with a story and leave the conclusion to the hearer. 'He who has ears to hear, let him hear.'

It was a time of terror and distress. The Israelites had arrived at the Red Sea. The waters were cold and deep and uninviting. Behind them a cloud of dust on the horizon signalled the pursuing chariots of the Egyptians. It was a time for decision.

One terror-stricken group decided to return to Egypt. 'Better to go back and live in bondage than to be massacred.' Another group decided that all was up and there was nothing for it but to jump into the sea and die. 'Better to drown than to die by the sword.' Another group was seething with anger as they cursed Moses and blasphemed God for landing them in this predicament.

The remaining group said, 'We'll go into the sea and go to the promised land.' They went into the sea and the water came up to their knees. As they advanced the water came up to their waists. They continued on and the water reached their chests. Soon they were in it up to their necks. They kept moving on and the water came to their mouths. And only then did God divide the waters.

3

The Three Story Model

God has a story too; and it is his story which is our real purpose in being. It is God's story in Torah and in Christ which is Gospel for the Christian.

JAMES A. SANDERS

It is really a matter of communication – getting the message across to the pews in the most effective way possible. Many years ago the Greek philosopher Aristotle wrote a book which he called *Rhetoric*. In it he laid down what many regard as the basic model of communication: the speaker, the message and the audience. The Church adopted this model and called it the preacher, God's message and the congregation. In our own times and particularly in the wake of the communications revolution with the new dimension of story and the fresh emphasis on the whole network of human experiences, the preacher has to deal with three sets of experiences in getting the message across Sunday after Sunday: his own, the ones of Jesus and those of his listeners. In the new homiletics the original model now becomes the story of the preacher, the story of God and the story of the listener. A word on each of these.

The Story of the Preacher. What we are determines the kind of message our hearers receive. The survey carried out by the Irish Liturgical Commission shows that what the majority of young people wanted to hear in the homily was the preacher's own story of faith. They expected the priest to give credible witness during the week to what he preached on Sunday.

In the document *On Evangelisation in the Modern World* Pope Paul VI describes the times we live in as one that 'thirsts for authenticity'. In it he is particularly sensitive to young people who 'have a horror of the artifical or false' and 'are searching above all for truth and honesty.' They are particularly alert to dishonesty in the pulpit.

'Father, your sermons terrify me,' said a lady to a priest, 'but your conduct consoles me.'

Talking about our own grace experience comes as a culture shock to many in my generation as we were told in our seminary days to avoid personal references or anything that savoured of narcissism or navel gazing. With good reason too because only too often has the pulpit been used as a platform for clerical idiosyncrasies and personal hang-ups, so much so that in many instances the story of God has gone untold.

The preacher who has himself been bruised by life can heal not from strength but from defeat. This is the theme of Henri Nouwen's book with the captivating title *The Wounded Healer*. The preacher who is himself a wounded healer brings an extra dimension of authenticity to his service.

One Saturday a young priest came to St Francis seeking advice and help with his Sunday sermon. Francis agreed and suggested that they both go for a walk together. As they strolled through the streets of Assisi Francis paused and gave alms to a family who were struggling to survive, their weekly income already well gone before they got it at all. Next he comforted a man imprisoned in a cell of loneliness through the death of his wife. Then he had a word with a couple whose marriage was falling apart, another who had just been told that he had an incurable illness. And so it went on until they arrived back at the monastery where Francis went to bid farewell to his guest.

'But Francis,' the priest exclaimed, 'you never helped me with my sermon.'

'Oh, but I did, Father,' the saint replied, 'I've just preached your sermon for you.'

The aim should be to tell our own story of faith in such a way that it illuminates the story of God and at the same time interacts with the stories of our people.

'I enjoy it when a priest talks about his own experience,' writes journalist Mary Kenny, 'last Christmas one of our local priests, Father Christopher Webb of Kensington, re-called his own childhood Christmases in which he finished by saying that the gift of the Christian faith which his parents had given to him was the greatest of all Christmas presents. This impressed my own children, I noticed' (*The Sower*, Autumn 1988).

The Story of God: Africans love stories. Long ago there was a storyteller in West Africa who was known as Ananse the Spiderman. His stories were woven on a native loom and they spoke of people, their joys and sorrows, their hopes and disappointments, their successes and failures. But the Spider-man had one abiding curiosity. He longed to know God's stories about his people. 'If I only knew', he sighed, 'the stories that God tells about us!' Then one day he spun a thread up into the sky right up to the throne of the Sky-God himself. God sat there and beside him was a golden box in which he kept all his stories about us. So impressed was he with the faith of Ananse that he gave him the box but instructed him not to open it until he returned to earth.

The Spiderman returned home, gathered the people, told them his story and then opened the box. In it was a book full of the stories of God beginning with the story of how he made the world and ending with a story about the heavenly home he had prepared for those who loved him. Every day the people came and listened to God's stories from the Good Book and Ananse, gifted storyteller that he was, sometimes re-told the stories of God in a fresh way to these particular people in these new times in which they were living. And as the people listened their lives were changed, their swords and spears were beaten into ploughshares and warring tribes merged into a community of love.

As we have seen preaching can never be the same again in the aftermath of the Second Vatican Council. When I compare my homilies today with the sermons I preached in the 1950s and 1960s what becomes most apparent is my changed approach to the Scriptures. In the early days I used it to prove points of doctrine. What was missing was personal experience of the word. The exegetes had taken away my Lord and I knew not where they had laid him. Now we are left with no choice but to proclaim the story of God – 'We do not speak in words taught by human wisdom but in words taught by the Spirit, as we explain spiritual truths to those who have the Spirit' (1 Cor 2:13). If we are to tell the story of God effectively we need to have a few basic convictions. Firstly, we need to re-assure ourselves that God has spoken, that he has communicated with his people by speech. Secondly, Scripture is God's word written down. Thirdly, God still speaks through what he has spoken; there is a contemporary voice of God with a contemporary message for modern man.

Finally, we need to convince ourselves that God's word is powerful, that when God speaks he acts, that his word can change people as it did in Shimbakuku. It happened in Okinawa towards the end of the Second World War. When American troops captured the island they found it in an appalling social and moral condition. Then one day they reached the village of Shimbakuku where they were greeted by two men, one of them carrying a Bible. Suspecting a trap they entered the village very cautiously – only to find it spotlessly clean, its fields tilled and fertile and everything a model of neatness and cleanliness in stark contrast to all the other villages roundabout. One of the old men gave them the reason. Thirty years earlier an American missionary on his way to Japan had called to Shimbakuku. He only stayed long enough to make two converts, the two old men. He taught them a few prayers and hymns, left them a Japanese translation of the Bible and urged them to live by it. With no other Christian contact and guided only by the Bible these two men transformed their community. There was no jail, no brothel, no drunkenness, no divorce; instead the people lived healthy, happy fulfilled lives – an oasis of love and purity in a desert of degradation.

Reader's Digest brought this amazing story to the attention of the world in a feature entitled 'Shimbakuku – the Village that Lives by the Bible', and Clarence Hall the war correspondent who first wrote the story summed up his feelings in the words of his dumbfounded driver, 'So this is what comes out of only a Bible and a couple of old men who wanted to live like Jesus! Maybe we're using the wrong kind of weapons to change the world.'

The Second Vatican Council has left us with no choice but to be steeped in the Scriptures. It tells us to read Scripture diligently and study it carefully lest any of us become 'an empty preacher of the word of God outwardly who is not a listener to it inwardly'. There is a crying need amongst us priests for continuing education particularly those of us who closed our last books in the seminary in the days before the Second Vatican Council. The new approach to Scripture makes it absolutely imperative that we keep in touch with the Church's understanding of revelation which is never a finished product. It goes on all the time and the trouble is – we've got to preach it. If not, what then do we preach?

The Story of the Listeners: I once heard a bishop say that if he were to re-state his episcopal motto his choice would be *Cognoscere Oves* – to know the sheep. Another bishop, Donal Murray of Dublin, points out 'The Good News can only be spoken from *within*. For a real understanding of the Gospel and for an effective preaching of it, therefore, one has to be, in some sense, one with the people to whom it is addressed – especially with the poor and the marginalised (but also with those for whom affluence and sophistication have brought a certain deafness).' Before the preacher can become a story-teller he must first be a story-listener. He must visit his people and listen to their stories of hope, fears, sorrow, bereavement, and in the light of what he hears be able to speak to their hungers. Wonderful moments of identification come in comments such as 'You were on my wave-length', 'You spoke my language', 'You could have been talking directly to me'.

It is interesting to note the variety of people who came to Jesus with all kinds of questions, how they should pray, what happens after death, should they pay tax, how often should they forgive, are those who suffer punished because of their sins? It is obvious that he knew his people. He could preach to them because he was one of them. 'Preaching,' said William Sangster, 'is the minister's effort to answer on Sundays the questions his people have been asking him during the week.'

In the old didactic style of preaching the sermon was a transfer of knowledge from the pulpit to the pew. The homily is an operation from faith to faith. I can only preach what I believe and I've got to persuade the people to believe what I believe. Faith, unlike knowledge, is a response of the whole person. If as a preacher I am looking for that kind of a response then what I say on Sundays must be closely related to the life and experience of my hearers. It calls for foot-slogging, the ringing of door bells rather then Church bells, it calls for being where the people are.

A perfect example of the Three Story Model where the preacher shared the story of God in a way that mirrored his own story and that of his listeners was a homily given in Warsaw by the murdered Polish priest, Jerzy Popieluszko. He told the story of Martin Luther King and reflected on three aspects of his life – bondage, exodus, promised land. His congregation immediately identified not only with the story of the civil rights leader but with the story in the Bible, the story of the preacher and their own story as well.

4

Stories for Re-telling

At its simplest the parable is a metaphor or simile drawn from nature or common life, arresting the hearer by its vividness or strangeness, and leaving the mind in sufficient doubt about its precise application to tease it into active thought.

C. H. DODD

An Egyptian folktale tells of a man long deceased who is miraculously re-incarnated as a child. He takes his father on a tour of the abode of the dead. There the old man is made to see the other side of two recent funerals. The scenario is meant to change the man's mind about life hereafter. What he sees first is a rich man who lived sumptuously, had a beautiful funeral but is now in torment. Then he sees a poor man who died unmourned, was buried in a pauper's grave but is now seated next to Osiris, the ruler of the abode of the dead clad in fine linen.

This folktale found its way into Jewish lore where Osiris was replaced by Abraham. Jesus, a storyteller in the Rabbinic tradition, re-tells the story in the parable of the Rich Man and Lazarus and in doing so adds a second part (vv27-32) about the five brothers. In the original story a man comes back from the dead and is able to convince a member of his family, but not so Lazarus. He cannot become a messenger. It is too late.

Jesus, a gifted storyteller, sees the creative possibilities in the original Cinderella-type story and embellishes it to give a timely warning to those of us who tend to resemble the five brothers, not necessarily bad, but just unconcerned about what is happening around us. The cardinal sin of our times is indifference. It dehumanises all of us. One is reminded of Studdart Kennedy's powerful poem:

When Jesus came to Golgotha they hanged him on a tree
They drove great nails through hands and feet and made a
    Calvary
They crowned him with a crown of thorns, red were his
    wounds and deep
For those were crude and cruel days and human flesh was
    cheap.

When Jesus came to Birmingham they simply passed him by
They never hurt a hair of him, they only let him die;
For men had grown more tender, and they would not give
    him pain:
They only just passed down the street, and left him in the rain.

Still Jesus cried, forgive them for they know not what they do,
And still it rained a wintry rain that drenched him through
    and through
The crowds went home and left the streets without a soul to
    see
And Jesus crouched against the wall, and cried for Calvary.

Like the re-telling of the Egyptian story Jesus' own stories were re-told in the early church for more than thirty years before they were written down. They were translated from Aramaic into Greek and those told in a Palestinian setting were re-told in and for a Hellenistic environment. Stories originally told to Jews were re-told to converted Christians and all the evidence is that the early church was somewhat creative in re-telling His stories. This creativity is strongly supported by the Biblical Commission's 'Instruction on the Historical Truth of the Gospels' (1964).

For many preachers today the parables of Jesus are histori-cally time-bound in a first century straitjacket, the sense of surprise is missing and seldom is the story 'teased into active thought'. With unremitting study of Scripture, the help of the exegete and listening to the stories of the people the preacher must shake the dust from the parables and make them live again. Sometimes when I hear the parable of the bridesmaids read at funeral masses (where it is a designated reading) I wonder what the mourners in the front seats make out of bridesmaids going out after dark with lanterns. Does the message of preparedness justify the medium of a first century marriage custom particularly in the context of a funeral? Or again take the illustration of the shepherd or the king and the kingdom. These concepts are light years away from the thinking of young people many of whom have never seen a flock of sheep grazing and have only heard that kings have been dethroned and kingdoms fallen.

The parables as Jesus told them were from real life: stories about farmers and fishermen, weddings and wakes, self righteous humbugs and prodigal sons, stories that related to the real life experiences of the Jews in the first century. The task confronting the preacher today is to break through the shackles of time and make the same stories relevant in the closing decades of the second millennium.

The Goban Saor was the greatest stone-mason of all time. This legendary figure is credited with building most of the ancient castles which dot the Irish countryside. Once, he received a commission from a chieftain to erect a castle so strong and impregnable that it would outshine all others. This he did and when the magnificent edifice was near completion, as the Goban was putting the finishing touches to the battlements, the chief had the scaffolding and ladders removed leaving the master craftsman stranded on the roof. He was determined that no one else would possess a castle to rival this one and the only way to ensure this was to get rid of the Goban. One day as the Goban languished on his lofty perch, he looked down and saw the village idiot staring up at him. 'Goban,' the fool shouted, 'how comes it that a smart man like you never heard that it is easier to throw down two

stones that to put one up. You're even a bigger fool than me.'
The Goban got the message and began throwing down the
stones until the chief got the message and gave him his
freedom.

The Goban lived less than two miles from the village
where I grew up in a place called The Island, a green patch of
land in the middle of a bog. The Island was once the site of an
old monastic settlement and the ruins of a mediaeval church
are still extant. I still have vivid memories of boyhood days
listening to an old lady in her nineties with a fund of stories
about the Goban. She solemnly assured me that he had
hidden his treasures on the Island. Forty years later a man
and his son walked the terrain with a metal detector and just
a few inches beneath where I had played as a boy they
discovered the now famous Derrynaflann chalice, currently
valued in millions!

Storytellers were very popular in Palestine and, like the
old lady on the Goban's Island, there was nothing people
liked more than a story of buried treasure. So they must have
been all ears when Jesus told them the stories of the treasure
hidden in the field and the pearl of great price. For centuries
people knew what it was to pack up in the middle of the night
and leave their farms and homesteads because of the threat-
ened invasion of some army on the march and quite often a
man would hastily bury his life's savings in the ground
hoping one day to come back and recover his wealth. More
often than not he never returned and it often happened that
someone years later stumbled upon an unexpected hidden
treasure.

So they latched on to Christ's story of the farmer whose
plough struck something hard in the ground which proved
to be an old chest full of coins and precious stones.

'Go on,' they said, 'tell us what happened next?' Now
notice the masterly way Jesus relates this story to the life
experience of those listening to him. Using compelling imagi-

nation he draws his hearers into his own faith experience. The sequence of finding, buying and selling was an authentic life experience for all of them so Jesus goes on: 'Because the price of the field was high the man had to sell everything he possessed in order to raise enough cash. But it was worth it. He just had to have that treasure.' The people got the point and no doubt some of them gave up their false gods of materialism and selfishness so that they could have instead the treasures of the kingdom of God.

Here again is the challenge to the preacher – using the dynamic of surprise, insight and a call to decision to make the parables speak again. Scratch and you will find little, dig deep and you will discover hidden treasure. The trouble is we talk about the treasure before experiencing it. If the treasure is a new relationship with God, then let's make room for it. This means letting go.

There's a well known story about a mountain climber who was on his way up a steep precipice when he lost his footing. Clinging to a jagged piece of rock he cried out in terror, 'O God, if you're up there please help me!' Then as he hung on for dear life he heard the voice of God. 'I will help you, but first of all you must let go!' The climber glanced at the yawning canyon stretching thousands of feet below and he called out again, 'Is there anyone else up there who can help?'

One of the truly great storytellers of modern times was the black preacher James Emmau Aggrey (1875-1927) of Ghana. A passionate advocate of civil rights and racial harmony he caused anxious moments for his followers by his outspokenness. But they need not have feared. 'I tell them a story, I get their mouths open for a laugh,' he said, 'and then I ram the truth down.' Here is his classic parable of the eagle:
'A certain man went through a forest seeking any bird of interest he might find. He caught a young eagle, brought it home and put it among his fowls and ducks and turkeys, and

gave it chicken's food to eat even though it was an eagle, the king of birds. Five years later a naturalist came to see him and, after passing through his garden said: "That bird is an eagle, not a chicken."

'"Yes," said its owner, "but I have trained it to be a chicken. It is no longer an eagle, it is a chicken, even though it measures fifteen feet from tip to tip of its wings."

'"No," said the naturalist, "it is an eagle still: it has the heart of an eagle, and I will make it soar high up to the heavens."

'"No," said the owner, "it is a chicken, and it will never fly."

'They agreed to test it. The naturalist picked up the eagle, held it up, and said with great intensity: "eagle you are an eagle; you belong to the sky and not to this earth; stretch forth your wings and fly." The eagle turned this way and that, and then looking down saw the chickens eating their food, and down he jumped.

'Then the owner said: "I told you it was a chicken."

'"No," asserted the naturalist, "it is an eagle, and it still has the heart of an eagle; only give it one more chance, and I will make it fly tomorrow."

'The next morning he rose early and took the eagle outside the city, away from the houses, to the foot of a high mountain. The sun was just rising, gilding the top of the mountain with gold, and every crag was glistening in the joy of that beautiful morning. He picked up the eagle and said to it: "Eagle you are an eagle; you belong to the sky and not to this earth; stretch forth your wings and fly!"

'The eagle looked round and trembled as if new life were coming to it; but it did not fly. The naturalist then made it look straight at the sun. Suddenly it stretched out its wings and, with the screech of an eagle, it mounted higher and higher and never returned. It was an eagle, though it had been kept and tamed as a chicken!'

And Aggrey's message: my people of Africa we were created in the image of God, but men have made us think that we are chickens and we still think we are, but we are eagles. Stretch forth your wings and fly! Don't be content with the food of chickens. This parable, limitless in its insights, is one that could have been put into the mouth of the Lord without blasphemy.

Soren Kierkegaard, the Danish philosopher and Lutheran Pastor compared his fellow Christians to domesticated geese. Those geese are always talking about flying: 'We have wings, we never use our wings, we should use them, let us fly!' But nobody ever flies. On Sundays a big goose stands a bit higher than the other ones on a pulpit, and he, too, every Sunday, exhorts the others in the most beautiful words, to fly. But nobody does fly, and if one would start to fly, the preacher would be the first one to shout: 'Come down immediately!'

This reminds one of the popular story of Jonathan Livingston Seagull, when Jonathan explains to the other seagulls that seagulls can live a much higher and fuller life than they do, the others did not believe him. When he shows them that it is really possible, they throw him out of their circle and ban him.

5

A Sledgehammer Introduction

Once upon a time, and a very good time it was. . .

JAMES JOYCE

'I usually switch off after one minute. . .' My attention arrested, I stopped in my tracks. It was a wedding reception and I had been moving about among the guests. There were four or five of them, their heads together in animated discussion trying to make themselves heard above the noise of the band. They were discussing sermons. 'Most people don't even give it a minute,' chimed in Keira, a pert young blonde from London, 'unless the opening line has a sledgehammer effect, I'm just not with it.' The music got louder and louder so to hear some more views from the pews I cornered Keira later in the relative quiet of the lounge. 'It was your talk in the church this afternoon that sparked off that discussion,' she said, 'As you know, you had a rather unusual mixture in your congregation.' She was correct. The groom was a playwright, his bride a set-designer, both creative artists, as were a number of their guests. 'It was imperative,' Keira went on, 'that you held our attention ... and you did with that sledgehammer introduction.' Keira works in communications and she drew an analogy from her own field. 'Television advertisers are experts at this,' she said, 'they have only thirty seconds in which to get their point across and they do it effectively. They know that unless they gain our attention they will not sell anything. You people have a lot to learn in this respect.'

The introduction is vital, because it is the means by which the thoughts of the preacher are got across to the pews in the shortest possible time. It requires careful thought and attention and, as a rule, should come last in the planning of a homily. Its function is to serve the theme of the message but this cannot be done unless we are clear in our minds about what the message will have as its main theme.

As we have seen, the introduction is an effective means of arresting the attention of the congregation. We should have a perceptive view of the pews as we approach the ambo and be conscious of what is hidden from our eyes. Attentive faces are no guarantee of attentive minds. The people's thoughts may be occupied with last night's television, with financial worries, a coming operation, an erring child or spouse or the afternoon ball-game. There is a moment of curiosity at the beginning. They do not know what you are going to talk about. 'This is your opportunity,' writes Denis Lane, 'to gain entrance, to fasten on that moment of curiosity, and to lead your hearers to think what you want them to think. Gain their attention now, and you may keep them for the whole message, lose their attention now and you may never get it back again.'

Creating opening lines such as the caption at the beginning of this chapter is an art form in itself, the art of condensing into the curtain-raiser the nub of the book or sermon. Classic examples of attention-gripping opening sentences are to be found in *Reader's Digest*. To begin a homily with fatuous statements like, 'Today is Easter Sunday' or 'The Gospel of today tells us...' is to invite inattention.There are many ways of introducing the homily such as statements that cause surprise, something that will make people curious or a question that creates interest. On one occasion when invited to preach in a Jesuit church, Tom Burke the famous Dominican preacher caused consternation in the pews and among his hosts when he began with 'To hell with the Jesuits.' After a pregnant pause he continued, 'That my friends is the cry of every rationalist in the world today.'

A story at the beginning would certainly get people's attention but we must ensure that it is brief and relevant to the theme. Some preachers get carried away by the story so much so that instead of introducing the message it becomes the main point of the homily. Do not always begin with a story because once people sense that you have a favourite way of introducing your subject they know what to expect to the detriment of the important elements of curiosity and surprise.

Finally, despite the wide range of thoughts that fill people's minds as we get up to speak let us not forget that there are still many people who come Sunday after Sunday hoping to get something from the Liturgy of the Word. They bring with them their anxieties, worries, hurts and hopes for a healing word, something that will lift them up, carry them on and give them the strength to bear the unhappiness they suffer at the present time. Being sensitive to their needs cannot but make us better preachers. A good introduction can be the bridge between the preacher and a message that will touch their souls.

6

Three Ways of Viewing God

*Nobody that I can remember throughout my educational days
ventured to preach a sermon on the Trinity; and I arrived at the start
of my Radio Pilgrimage with the nicely polished witticism that the
doctrine of the Trinity was like the Victorian piano in the front
parlour; nobody played it nowadays, but nobody dared throw it out.*

GERALD PRIESTLAND

In a scene in Helen Waddell's biography of Peter Abelard
one of Abelard's students, Pierre de Montboissier comes in a
distressed state to Gilles de Vannes, Canon of Notre Dame.
A fire has been prepared to burn Abelard's book on the
Trinity which has been condemned as heretical. It is beyond
the comprehension of the young man that the work of his
hero, the brilliant Abelard should be regarded as heretical.
Gilles comforts Pierre by reminding him that every book that
was ever written about the Trinity had been condemned as
heretical barring the Athanasian Creed. 'And even that,' he
added, 'only saves itself by contradicting everything it says
as fast as it says it.'

Part of the problem in preaching on the Trinity is the
jargon of the theologians, the manner in which it was presented to us in our seminary days. We were subjected to a
barrage of philosophising on abstruse terms like essence,
substance, subsistence, relations, processions, all terribly
remote from the simple manner in which this basic mystery
of the Christian faith is understood by Lena, my house-
keeper. 'They're all the one and that's it!'

Once a young priest fresh from the seminary treated a simple rural congregation to a learned dissertation on the processions in the Trinity. A little old lady came to him after Mass, 'that was a grand sermon, Father, but you never told us what time does the procession start!'

On one occasion when a bishop was administering the Sacrament of Confirmation in a city parish he drew the attention of one of the candidates to a stained glass window depicting the baptism of Christ. The young hopeful had just assured the prelate that there were three persons but only one God. The bishop pointed to the figure of Christ in the waters of the Jordan and asked, 'Is he God?'

Getting an affirmative he pointed to the Holy Spirit hovering over the head of Christ.

'And him?' he queried.

'He's God too,' came the confident response.

Ticking off two fingers the bishop now turned the boy's attention to the Father in the clouds, 'What about him?'

'Yeah, I reckon he's God as well.'

'Doesn't that make three Gods?' said the bishop holding up three fingers.

'No, one God,' the boy was adamant.

'But I don't understand' mused the bishop still gazing at the window.

The aspiring soldier of Christ looked at the bishop somewhat tolerantly and then produced his trump card – 'But you're not supposed to understand. Can't you see it's a mystery!'

And that's the crux for the preacher. For too long it has been a mystery, the toy of the theologians and clouded in their jargon. It is the central truth of our faith, the very core of the Christian religion and it has to be got across to the pews in such a way that it will touch the lives of those who listen to us Sunday after Sunday.

A. M. Hunter has this very perceptive comment on what

he calls the underpinning realities. 'If you had asked St Paul what were the ultimate realities that underpinned his life, he would have answered, "Why, the grace of the Lord Jesus Christ and the love of God, and the fellowship of the Holy Spirit."' This approach would appear to be tailor-made for the homilist with a flair for using three points in his homily. An even simpler approach would be the Trinitarian gesture which has become the trade-mark of our faith, the Sign of the Cross.

Chambers' Dictionary defines the verb 'to illustrate' as 'to make bright, to adorn... to make clear to the mind, to explain, to adorn with pictures.' All illustrations have their limitations. There is no illustration existing that can light up the truth of the Trinity, for the truth of God in his innermost being is beyond human comprehension and analysis. In trying to make it understandable some preachers use the illustration of the sun. We can look at the sun but cannot see it, what we do see is its brightness. We cannot see God but we can see Jesus Christ in whom the Father's glory and brightness is revealed.

We speak of feeling the sun on our bodies whereas it is not the sun but the heat and the warmth of the sun that we experience. Similarly although the Holy Spirit is invisible we can experience the power and warmth of his presence in our lives. The sun whose brightness we see and whose heat we feel is one sun, not three. This illustration has proven useful in shedding light on the Trinity but then there is an obvious draw back. The sun is not a person!

The story is told that St Augustine once set himself the task of solving the mystery of how three persons really distinct and equal in all things could possess the one divine nature. He would get up early in the morning when the mind was fresh and uncluttered and walk by the sea pondering on the ultimate realities. One morning as he strolled by the shore he saw to his surprise a child all alone digging a hole in the sand with a tiny shovel. He approached the child and asked him the purpose of his digging. 'As soon as I've dug this hole I'm going to empty the sea into it,' was the reply.

'But child,' said Augustine, 'look at the vast expanse of sea. How might I ask are you going to empty it into that tiny hole?'

The child looked up at him and replied, 'Sooner than you will empty the vastness of God into your tiny little mind.'

Augustine went home and gave up trying to unravel the mystery.

There is a story about a Jew who had a sudden heart attack on the street. A priest appeared on the scene, knelt by the victim and asked if he were a Christian. The Jew looked perplexed.

'Do you believe in the Trinity,' persisted the priest, 'you know the three in one?'

'My God,' grasped the stricken Jew, 'at a time like this... at a time like this all he can offer me is a mathematical proposition!'

7

On the Side of the Angels

I will send an angel ahead of you to protect you as you travel and to bring you to the place which I have prepared.

Exodus 23:20

There's a story of a priest who used to spend hours everyday preparing his Sunday homily. His congregation was small, so sparse in fact that in the considered view of his house-keeper it did not warrant the painstaking efforts he put into preaching to them. On one occasion as he worked on his sermon far into the night she interrupted him: 'Will you go to bed and don't be wasting your time on that lot. Don't you know well that you'll only have a few listening to you?'

'Ah yes,' he replied, 'but think of the vast audience who will be there.'

If he included angels in his grandstand, and I suspect he did, when I read of their spectator role in 1 Cor 4:9, then I am in real trouble. I have never preached on angels nor for that matter have I ever listened to a sermon on them. Why then am I now embarking on relatively unchartered territory? Perhaps it's to ease my conscience because the whole subject bothers me. Let me just share three points.

I've got to be concerned with them because they are very much a part of the Eucharistic celebration I offer daily. We refer to them at the beginning of Mass when we ask 'all the angels and saints and you my brothers and sisters to pray for me to the Lord our God.' In the Creed we profess our faith in a God who created '. . . all that is seen and unseen' and as we approach the solemn moment of consecration we tell the Father that we 'join the angels and saints in proclaiming your glory.' Do we really have that sense of joining with the angels at Mass? Indeed I am still young enough to remember when the final prayer of the Mass was a plea to Michael 'Prince of the Heavenly host to cast down to hell Satan and with him all other wicked spirits who wander through the world seeking the ruin of souls.'

Secondly, we can know nothing of angels apart from revelation so the old mediaeval debate of how many of them could dance on the point of a needle is both foolish and irrelevant. The Scriptures abound with references to angels, almost three hundred in all. They are in the *Book of Genesis* at the beginning and in the *Book of Revelation* at the end. We read how Abraham entertained them in his tent; how one of them stayed his hand when he was about to sacrifice Isaac; how Jacob wrestled with one of them one lonely night in the gorge of Jabbok. Moses was encompassed by ten thousand angels on Sinai and one of them came to Daniel not merely to deliver him from the lions but to show him what God foresaw would happen to the world. They appear as God's agents in the destruction of Sennacherab and above all in the destruction of the Egyptian first-born at the first Jewish Passover. Turning to the *New Testament*, God sends them as his messengers to make special announcements for him. Gabriel comes to Zecharias to announce the birth of John the Baptist and in the most momentous mission of all to Mary to proclaim the coming of the Redeemer. He comes to Joseph to tell him to take Mary as his wife; angels are present in the shepherd's field at the Nativity, in Gethsemane, at the Cross, the empty tomb and again at the Ascension. They delivered Peter from prison, visited John on Patmos and the same John in his *Book of Revelation* speaks of them in thousands.

In the face of all this evidence from the Scriptures where they occupy a far more important place than does Satan, isn't it strange that there is so much interest in demonology in the world today. Works on Satan and Satanism stare at us from bookshelves, newsstands, libraries and video-shops. Satan has had his innings. How about turning to the angels!

Finally, what about Guardian Angels? Do the angels influence our lives 'to light and guard, to rule and guide' as the old prayer reminds us? Strange as it may seem the Church has never defined as an article of faith that each of us has a Guardian Angel but there is a long tradition which claims that we have. The Guardian Angels have a special feast to themselves on 2 October. The idea of a Guardian Angel underpins the basic Christian belief in God's special love and concern for each one of us. The Psalmist reminds us that 'God will put his angels in charge of you to protect you wherever you go' (Ps 91:11). Islamic theologians claim that two angels are assigned to each person, one to record the good deeds, and one the bad.

There are quite a few stories about the recording angel. One I like tells of one of the Desert Fathers who spent his life away from the world in prayer and fasting. Everyday he would trudge one mile across the hot sands to draw water from a well. Advancing years made the task more arduous and bothersome so one day as he plodded back along the sands with his bucket of water he decided that on the morrow he would move his tent nearer to the well. No sooner had he made his decision than he heard a voice behind him. It was counting. When he stopped the counting stopped. Turning around he saw an angel standing behind him.

'Carry on,' said the heavenly visitor. 'I am just counting your tortuous steps so that none of them will go without its reward.'

That night the holy man shifted his tent another mile further away from the well!

One day perhaps like the holy man the scales will fall from our eyes and we will see the full extent of the role the angels have played in our lives. 'What we see now is like a dim image in a mirror; then we shall see face to face. What I know now is only partial; then it will be complete – as complete as God's knowledge of me' (1 Cor 13:12).

There's a story about a person who was walking down the street and saw an angel coming towards him with a torch in one hand and a bucket of water in the other. When he asked what the angel planned on doing with the torch and bucket, the angel replied, 'I'm going to set fire to the mansions of heaven with the torch and I'm going to quench the fire of hell with the bucket of water. Then we'll see who really loves God.'

Then there's the story of the angel sent on a 'mission impossible'. It centres on two shopkeepers situated across the street from each other and such was the cut-throat competition between them that they grew to hate each other. They were constantly peering across the street to see which of them had the more attractive display of goods and who had the more customers. To win one of the rival's customers was an occasion for celebration. When their mutual animosity got to the stage where their children were not on speaking terms the Lord decided to step in. He sent one of his most skilled negotiators, the Archangel Raphael with instructions to sort the sorry situation out.

The angel approached one of the antagonists and told him about the Lord's concern. 'Look,' he said to the shopkeeper, 'I've been authorised to tell you that you can have anything you wish, the finest supermarket with the very latest business technology, a booming trade, security for the rest of your life. . . you just name it and it's yours.'

The man was rubbing his hands gleefully when the angel went on, 'There's just one condition attached to the deal. Your rival across the way will be given double of whatever you request.'

The shopkeeper thought it over for a while, looked venomously across the street, then turning to the angel said, 'Right, you just go back to the Lord, and ask him to make me blind in one eye!'

Once the devil disguised as an angel of light came to a holy man in the desert and said, 'I am an angel of God and have been sent to you by the Lord.'

The holy man replied, 'Think again, you must have been sent to someone else. I've done nothing to deserve the visit of an angel.'

The devil left him.

Jews and Christians are at one in the worship of the One True God. They also share another priceless possession – the first five books of the Bible known to Christians as the *Pentateuch* and sacred to the Jews as the *Torah*. According to Jewish lore when Moses went up to Heaven to receive the *Torah* from God he encountered jealousy and opposition from the angels. Outraged to find a mortal in the celestial abode they voiced their protest to God and they were even more indignant when they learned the purpose of Moses' visit.

'Lord!' they exclaimed, 'how can you hand over to man this priceless jewel which we have treasured for 974 generations before you created the world. What is man, that you think of him' (Ps 8:40). And God commanded Moses to answer the case brought forward by the angels.

'Lord of the Universe,' replied Moses, 'let me remind the angels of what is written in the *Torah* which you intended to give to me: "I am the Lord your God who brought you out of Egypt, where you were slaves" (Exodus 20:2). O Angels, have you ever gone down to Egypt? Do you know what it is to be a slave? Then why should the Lord give you the *Torah*? Again what else is written in the *Torah*?: "You shall have no other gods before me." Are you living among heathens that you should serve other gods? "You shall not take a false oath" – Are you engaged in business that you should be commanded not to take a false oath? Furthermore, "Honour your father and your mother." Have you a father and mother that you should be commanded to honour them? "You shall not kill, you shall not commit adultery, you shall not steal." Is there envy and hatred among you that you should be commanded not to do these things? Of what good then is the *Torah* to you?'

When the angels heard this they changed their tune and became friendly to Moses and each one of the angels taught him something, even the angel of death.

8

A Question of Justice

I sit on a man's back, choking him, and making him carry me, and yet assure myself and others that I am very sorry for him and wish to ease his lot by any means possible, except getting off his back.

LEO TOLSTOY

In John Steinbeck's *The Grapes of Wrath* there's a dramatic scene where the small holdings of the poor in Oklahoma are being taken over by the 'fifty thousand acre monster' – the bank. One of the tenants about to be evicted has a problem. It is a simple one or perhaps not quite so simple. The problem is: who does he shoot? 'Grampa killed the Indians,' he cries, 'Pa killed snakes for the land. Maybe we can kill banks – they're worse than Indians and snakes.' He tries to find out who gave the orders to turn him off the land and traces it back to the President of the bank. So he decides to fill up the magazine of the rifle and go into the bank. Then he's told that the bank gets orders from the east. The orders are: 'Make the land show profit or we'll close you up.'

'But where does it stop?' he cries in exasperation, 'who can we shoot? I don't aim to starve to death before I kill the man that's starving me.'

Recently, the Dublin priest Michael Cleary took on a bank for introducing 'cheap labour' by giving the young unemployed sub-standard wages. He described the bank as a 'monster' indulging in a cynical gesture in giving 'dead-end jobs' to young people in its ruthless pursuit of profit. His stricture, if correct, is a symptom of the malaise affecting the economic structure of the western world today. Man's current pursuit of profit and progress which promotes multinational companies and increased specialisation has in fact resulted in an enormous cost in human terms, massive unemployment, environmental pollution and inhumane working conditions. Carrick-on-Suir is a town in County Tipperary not far from my own parish. A few weeks ago, eight priests went there to give a three weeks mission. During the first week they visited the homes where they listened to the stories of the people. What they heard and witnessed shocked them. Here was a community ravaged by unemployment, poverty and emigration. The priests went public on 'the shameful treatment of these people' and pointed an accusing finger at the politicians with their obsession for fiscal rectitude and reducing the taxes of the better-off. By entering into solidarity with the poor these priests were in a position to preach the all inclusive love of God with conviction for the remainder of the mission. This was the kind of preaching that Jesus was engaged in, 'bringing the good news to the poor.' He abhorred the dehumanising oppression of the poor and the world of power, prestige and possessions which the rich had constructed for them.

In bringing the good news to the poor we have to preach a message that will make people uncomfortable especially as the pews are the only forum left to us where the oppressor and the oppressed sit side by side. We are constantly confronted with disturbing statistics about the Third World – 45,000 children dying of malnutrition every day and two-thirds of the worlds population going to bed hungry every night. These frightening facts must make us feel uncomfortable. However right under our noses on Sunday there are glaring instances of injustice and oppression. Beatrice is a case in point. Beatrice is a widow. She and her husband ran a successful business until he died in his forties. Beatrice was left with a young family and she was owed thousands of pounds. However the creditors refused to pay up and she had to sell the business and go to work to meet her own bills and support her children. A short time ago she came to me and vented her frustration. 'I feel like giving up going to Mass,' she said, 'I just can't pray when I see them driving to the church in their new cars. They sit beside me in the pew in all their finery, they march up to Holy Communion and these are the very ones who forced me to sell out and go to work. When are you going to get back to basics in your preaching. When are you going to stand up there and give a sermon on the seventh commandment and tell them to pay their debts. Believe me it is long overdue.'

I did believe her and decided to do something about it but first I dug out what was the standard text-book of theology in every Irish home when we were growing up, the old Butler Catechism. The pages were now yellow with age and as I leafed through them memories were evoked of how this little book had once blighted the prospect of what should have been for me a promising criminal career.

It all began when I got involved in a protection racket. I had to pay out to shield myself from the unwelcome attentions of a gang of toughs who were a few years my senior. I was only eleven at the time and my mother ran a small grocery shop in the village where I grew up. Unknown to her and at her expense I bribed myself into the good books of the gang by pilfering sweets and chocolate bars. As I became more adept at petty thieving the lure of the cash register became more and more inviting so I carefully plotted the big-time robbery. One morning, when the house was quiet and the shop empty I crept stealthily to the till and as I relieved it of half a crown – an enormous sum in those days – I was caught red-handed. 'Give me that money you young thief,' my mother shrieked retrieving her hard-earned coin from my grasp. Then with an ominous 'You just wait until your father comes home.' I was banished to the bedroom, where I spent the day in solitary confinement and fearful expectation of the wrath to come.

When my father returned he was briefed on the misdemeanour and in fear and trepidation I braced myself for the thud of his footsteps on the stairs and the inevitable punishment. To my surprise I was left in solitary confinement, my only sustenance being a mug of tea and a slice of dry bread which were pushed inside the door. That night the conversation in my parents bedroom went on into the early hours. I crept to the door and caught snatches of it like, 'I'm telling you Tom, if we don't do something he'll bring disgrace down on top of us,' to which Dad replied, 'We'll see in the morning. Go to sleep, woman!'

The following day I was greeted by stony silence. It was Saturday and my Sunday suit was airing in front of the fire. Shortly after midday I was told to get dressed and packed into the Baby Ford which was Dad's pride and joy but not so today. The silence in the car was oppressive as we drove the eight miles to Thurles. The car came to a halt outside the cathedral and as Dad left for the nearest hostelry to drown his sorrows my mother pushed me unceremoniously into the darkness of the huge church. Mid-way up the side-aisle she planted me down beside her on a seat and there the two of us awaited our turn to go to Confession. She went in first and was so long in the box that I thought to myself that she had many sins to confess never suspecting that the priest was being well and truly briefed on my criminal activities. As I waited for her to emerge my eyes wandered round the vast edifice. I counted the windows – twenty-one lighted the apse and ten each of the aisles. Over the windows and supporting the roof were shafts of white, red and green marble with sculptured capitals resting on corbels representing the heads of the saints. There were twenty-eight heads in all. Later I was to learn that these heads were the expression of an idea that the Church of Christ reposes on the saints as its principal mainstays but today all twenty-eight of them seemed to be glaring down at me and shouting: Thief! thief!

Cowering beneath their accusing countenances I was finally rescued by my mother who piloted me into the penitent's section. As she closed the door leaving me in the darkness her face resembled those of the saints only hers was a countenance more in sorrow than in anger. I decided to get the ordeal over as quickly as possible so as soon as the priest pulled the slide I launched into my usual formula: Bless me father... I cursed; I told lies, I was disobedient, I stole... O my God I am heartily sorry...' to be halted by the voice from the inner sanctum, 'Just a minute. . . just a minute, what did you steal?'

'Money and sweets, Father, but... but it was at home.'

'So you think it's not a sin to steal from your parents! Well sonny I have some news for you.' Then he proceeded to give me a roasting. He told me that I was a budding criminal and that like all criminals I was beginning my life of crime at home; that I would come to a bad end unless I amended my evil ways and that I would bring shame and disgrace on my parents who were 'dragging and slaving' to bring me up right and decent. He finished his tirade by giving me an enormous penance. I was to say a full rosary! After a rather peremptory absolution and dismissal I emerged from the tribunal licking my wounds. The saints from their lofty pedestals seemed to be leering down at me and saying, 'I told you so, I told you so!' The one real saint in my life, my mother, was much more conciliatory. She told me to be a good boy in the future and then pressed sixpence into my hand. That experience had two salutary effects. Never again did I dare to take anything that was not mine and never again did I set foot in that dark tribunal in Thurles Cathedral, never, that is, until twenty-five years later when by a strange and ironic twist of providence it was to be my penitentiary for twenty years, this time as confessor and judge.

Why have I told you this story? Well, some time ago, I used it in abbreviated form, to introduce a homily on the seventh commandment. Afterwards a lady came to me and said, 'Thank God you're human like ourselves.' It was a magical moment of indentification! The story has an epilogue, so bear with me!

When we arrived home after the Cathedral inquisition my

father took me aside and put a small book into my hands which turned out to be the Butler Catechism, 'Read that... out loud,' he ordered pointing to a question and answer on the seventh commandment. With trembling voice I stumbled through the answer: 'We are commanded by the seventh commandment to pay our lawful debts, to give every man his own and they who retain ill-gotten goods or who have unjustly what belongs to another are bound to restore them as soon as possible and as far as they are able, otherwise the sin will not be forgiven.' Then he sat me down and scorched into my memory the implications of what I had just read, that stealing brought with it an obligation to make restitution, not merely an intention but a serious effort; otherwise the sin will not be forgiven – that if I did not pay back what I had stolen the sin would be like a millstone around my neck which I would carry with me to the Day of Judgment. 'Never forget the seventh commandment!' he finally admonished. I felt that I had just been subjected to a giant x-ray revealing the bone structure of my sinfulness.

I was later to learn that if charity begins at home so also does justice. Husbands who do not hand over an adequate share of the pay-packet or who squander on drink or gambling what is due in justice to the family are the chief offenders in this area, as also are wives trying to keep up with the Jones through improvident spending. Young people too are not immune from guilt when they fail to contribute to the family budget. How seldom, if ever, do family members accuse themselves of transgressions such as these.

About eight-hundred years before Christ there was a small farmer called Amos who looked after a few sheep and goats on his bit of land near Bethlehem. What made him special and different from the farmers and shepherds around him was that he was a prophet. Now a more unlikely prophet than Amos it would be hard to find. He never wanted the job but still God called him to deliver an important message to

the people of his time. They were a people much like ourselves, outwardly religious, regular church-goers and great
for going on pilgrimages. Four times a year they would head
for Jerusalem on pilgrimage and on the way they would pass
Amos' little plot chanting their hymns and psalms and
canticles to God. In Jerusalem they would offer their sacri-
fices of expiation, praise and thanksgiving to the Lord. But
despite this outward show of religion there was rampant
dishonesty everywhere. Farmers were fiddling, shopkeepers were giving short measures, everyone was after the quick
buck. Their religion was a gigantic fraud. And so God sent
Amos to them as his mouthpiece and this was his message:

> I hate... I reject your pilgrimages;
> I am not pleased with your sacred ceremonies.
> When you present your sacrifices and offerings
> I will not accept them;
> I don't want to hear your hymns
> I can't endure your music.
> Though you offer countless prayers
> I will not listen
> Let justice roll on like a river!

If Amos came back today what would he have to say to
some of the best church-going people in the world? First of
all he'd be surprised to find that an Eleventh Commandment
had been added to the decalogue: 'Thou shalt not get caught.'
Any way of getting goods is all right as long as you can get
away with it. So its OK to lift the firms' property, pilfer in the
supermarket, draw money for work not done, fiddle with the
dole, evade income-tax, provided of course that you can get
away with it. Amos would be shocked to learn that some of
the best church-going people would not regard these as
stealing.

If Amos stood in one of our modern-day pulpits would he
perhaps point an accusing finger at the pews and say, 'I
hate...I reject your Sunday Eucharist because you are making

no effort to pay your debts, because by not paying your debts you are imposing hardship on others; I hate your daily Masses because you are an oppressor who will not pay a living wage; I will not listen to your prayers because you are not putting in an honest day's work, because you are fiddling on the job, because you are pilfering in the shops, because you are spending foolishly and living beyond your means.'

Would he enter some of our Catholic homes and point an accusing finger at the husbands: you are breaking the seventh commandment of God because you are squandering on drink and gambling what is due in justice to your wife and family? Would he say to the wives: you too are at fault because you are piling up debts and neglecting the home? Would he perhaps then turn on young people and accuse them of not rowing in with their share of the family budget by excessive spending on drink, discos and cigarettes?

Strong language, you might say! Well, the Lord did not consider it too strong when he put it into the mouth of his prophet to denounce with scorching wrath and burning indignation a worship that was divorced from Christian living.

When Willie was a small child he was with his father when he was stopped for speeding. He saw his father slipping a ten pound note with his licence to the policeman. 'It's all right, son,' said his Dad driving off, 'they all do it.'

Sometime later he was in the supermarket with his mother who received wrong change as they passed through the check-out. As she put the extra cash into her handbag she said, 'It's OK Willie, everyone does it.' Willie got a summer job in the fruit department of the same supermarket. One of his jobs was to put the over-ripe tomatoes at the bottom of the box and the more presentable ones on the top. 'It's good for business, son,' his boss told him,

Later on in life Willie got a good job as financial controller in a textile company. He was caught fiddling the books and dismissed. When he returned home in ignominy his parents upbraided him: 'Look at the shame and disgrace you have brought upon us. If there is anything we cannot stand, it is dishonesty.'

Thieves meet with rough justice in Islamic countries. They have their hands chopped off. In one state where the penalty for stealing was death by hanging a young man was caught in the act of stealing a loaf of bread. On the eve of his execution he was granted a final request. He told the ruler that he would like to plant an orange seed at the place of execution and that the tree would yield fruit overnight. His father had given him the secret. The following day the ruler, his ministers and the populace gathered in the marketplace. A hole was dug and the thief was about to plant the seed when he hesitated. 'This seed,' he said addressing the ruler, 'can only be sown by someone who has never stolen anything if it is to grow and bear fruit overnight. I am a convicted thief, so I cannot plant it.'

The ruler signalled to his justice minister but the minister said, 'I can remember taking some sweets from a shop when I was a child, so I cannot plant the seed.'

The chief of police was summoned and he recalled stealing apples when he was a teenager.

Even the ruler was thinking to himself, I remember keeping something that belonged to my father.

The young man turned to his accusers. 'Here are you, the chief men in the realm, each one of you is guilty of stealing and here am I who stole a little food to stay alive and I am to be hanged.'

Pleased with the man's wisdom, the ruler pardoned him.

A priest once decided to offer his own modernised version of the Ten Commandments. They went like this:

Remember that thou goest easy in the evil necessity of work.

Five days mayest thou labour with every possible rest for tea.

On the sixth or seventh thou mayest do overtime, double rates, for this is the covenant with the union.

On the seventh day thou canst please thyself about bed or sport or washing thy car and read the Sunday newspapers.

The Trade Union preferred the version Moses brought down from the mountain and reported him to his bishop.

9

Telling Love Stories

God may well be loved, but not thought. By love may he be gotten and holden, but by thought never.

THE CLOUD OF UNKNOWING

The difficulty with this story is where to begin. The world of Bernadette Nolan lay in pieces when she discovered that her child was born with brain damage. If he lived he would be mute, have no control over any of his limbs and be confined to a wheelchair all his life. It would not be easy to take care of him but Bernadette was determined that she would. Every day she massaged his entire body; she prayed over him; she cried over him; she placed his crippled hands in her tears. As he grew so did Bernadette's problems. He needed twenty-four hour supervision and time and again she was advised to place him in an institution. Had she done so the world would never have come to know the glittering talent of Christopher Nolan.

Bernadette continued to love him and to pray with him. She told him stories of God and read to him from the classics even though he didn't seem to hear her; she surrounded him with music and conversation; she introduced him to the beauty of nature and in the summer plunged his body into the running waters of streams and rivers.

Then she and her husband bought an electric typewriter. She strapped a unicorn stick to his forehead and cradling his head in her hands taught him to stab at the letter keys. She coaxed and cajoled him, sometimes standing for fourteen

hours a day holding his head and hoping that the words
would come. The family moved to Dublin so that Christy
could be near the Central Remedial Clinic. A new drug was
found to relax his muscles and then on 20 August 1977 as
Bernadette again held his head her labour of love was
rewarded as she watched the words of a poem trickle on to
the page of a typewriter. He called it 'I learn to bow.' It was
just one of dozens of poems which he had written in his head
over the past eight years. He was just eleven years old. By the
time he was fifteen all his poems were on paper and his first
book *Damburst of Dreams* appeared in 1981. Six years later
came the autobiographical *Under the Eye of the Clock* which
won him the Whitbread Award, one of the world's most
prestigious literary prizes. 1988 saw the production of his
first play. Christy Nolan, thanks to a mother's faith and love,
is now an acknowledged literary genius.

The Greeks had a word for the astonishing love of Bernadette Nolan. They called it *agape*. The word 'love' in the
English language just about describes everything from
Heaven to Hollywood. It is used of God giving himself to us
in his Son; of Christ's giving of himself for us on the cross; of
a man and woman giving themselves to each other in copu-
lation; of Mother Teresa giving herself to the destitutes in
Calcutta; of the queer shenannigans at folk-festivals and it is
bandied about in erotic literature, pop-songs and video
nasties.

The Greek language in which the *New Testament* is written
is more subtle than English and has three words which we
translate as love. First there is *eros* which survives in our
word erotic and means sexual love. Of the three Greek words
for love this is the only one not used by the *New Testament*
writers. Secondly, there is *philia* meaning friendship. You
will find it just once in the *New Testament*. But the word used
by Paul in his great song of songs (1 Cor 13) is *agape*. This
agape is the highest expression of love known to mankind.
John uses it to tell us that God is love and that love comes
from God. It is used throughout the *New Testament* to

describe personal relationship, our relationship with God and neighbour. It is a caring unselfish love, a love of giving, a love which is able to endure hardship and suffering and which finds its fullest expression on the cross.

Love in its Christian meaning is more than sexual desire (*eros*), more than liking (*philia*) for the source of *agape* is not human emotions or sentiments, but according to St John the very being of God himself. 'If,' says A. M. Hunter, 'eros is all take and philia is give and take, agape is all give.' These three indicators of love's presence need to be mentioned in our homilies from time to time if only to allay some of the confusion that exists over this underpinning reality of our Christian faith.

Here is a story of pure love from the days of the cultural revolution in Red China.

A pastor and two Christian girls were sentenced to death. As on many other occasions in Church history, the persecutors mocked them. They promised to release the pastor if he would shoot the girls. He accepted.

The girls waited in the prison yard for the announced execution. A fellow-prisoner who watched the scene from his prison cell described their faces as pale but beautiful beyond belief; infinitely sad but sweet. Humanly speaking, they were fearful, but they decided to submit to death without renouncing their faith. Then, flanked by guards, the executioner came with a revolver in his hand: it was their own pastor. The girls whispered to each other, then bowed respectfully before the pastor. One of them said: 'Before being shot by you, we wish to thank you heartily for what you have meant to us. You baptised us, you taught us the way of eternal life, you gave us Holy Communion with the same hand in which you now have the gun. May God reward you for all the good you have done us. You also taught us that Christians are sometimes weak and commit terrible sins, but they can be forgiven again. When you regret what you are about to do to us, do not despair like Judas, but repent like

Peter. God bless you, and remember that our last thought was not one of indignation against your failure. Everyone passes through hours of darkness. We die with gratitude.'

They bowed again. They knew it was the Lord who had provided that suffering should come when they would feel it most: in the betrayal of their pastor.

The pastor's heart was hardened. He shot the girls. Afterwards he himself was shot by the Communists. This happened in Kiangsi.

On his thirteenth birthday, a young Indian brave was placed in the middle of a large jungle, and told to spend the night there, as a test of nerve and bravery before being accepted into young manhood in the tribe. It was a long, long night. Every leaf that fell, every branch that creaked, every creature that moved in the undergrowth, caused a shiver of fear to pass through him. He never knew a night could be so long; there was no hope of sleep, and, more than once, he was on the verge of running away. Finally, after what seemed like ages, the dawn began to filter through the trees, and slowly his vision adjusted to the growing light. As he peered around, he was really surprised to see his father standing behind the nearest tree, gun in hand. He had been on guard there all night! The boy's first thoughts were, 'If I had known that my father was standing on guard like that, I would have slept soundly all night!'

When I die, and express any surprise at how my Father had watched over me in life, Jesus could surely say, 'But I told you that! That was the very reason I came. The night of life need not have been so anxious after all!'

The great American storyteller O. Henry wrote about a young married couple Jim and Della who were poor but very much in love. It was Christmas Eve and they wanted to give presents to each other. Having no money to buy presents, each one, without telling the other, decided to sell his or her most precious possession. Della's most precious possession was her long golden hair and she went to a hairdressers and had it cut off. She sold it to buy a chain for a watch which had been left to Jim by his father. She came home and found Jim awaiting her. Looking at her his eyes were filled as he handed her his gift. It was a set of beautiful combs. He had sold his watch to purchase them for her. There was no hair for the combs and no watch for the chain. But they were left with something more precious – *agape*, their self-sacrificing love for each other.

Daniel Corkery has an enchanting story about a poor old man in a shabby lodging-house in the city. People sometimes spoke of him as The Child; at other times they called him The Saint. One name was as apt as the other; in spite of the squalid environment in which he lived, he was a saint; in spite of his age, a child. His room was filled with objects of devotion; of other furniture there was little or none. He had several pictures of the Blessed Virgin, a few of the Holy Family, many of the better known saints – St Patrick, St Joseph, St Anthony. He had several statues and he kept a supply of holy water in a little chinaware font which a chinaware angel kneeling, upheld. Amongst these, his treasures, he lived alone in quiet ecstasy speaking much to himself and to them too on occasions.

He knew that the Phelan family on the lower landing were in trouble. His hand catching his door he listened to the rent-collector's voice growing louder and angrier as he served a notice-to-quit on Mrs Phelan. The Child stumbled down the stairs crying 'Give her till tomorrow... give her till tomorrow.' After some persuasion the agent reluctantly agreed and left muttering, 'Tomorrow then, not one day later.'

The Child returned to his room, took up his chinaware angel and having emptied the holy water into a bottle dusted the figure and put it into a bag. Then he climbed up on the bed and took down his favourite picture, a beautiful portrait of the Blessed Virgin. Into the tail pocket of his coat he put a small painted plaster statue of St Anthony. Then taking the picture, with great difficulty he made his way down the narrow stairs. The shining angel with golden curls peeped out of his bag as he shuffled his way to the market-place where his friend Mrs McCarthy was selling her wares from a mobile barrow. She undertook to sell the pious objects for him as he sat on one of her stools.

The chinaware angel was the first to go. As the purchaser, a poor lady was about to leave he said to her, 'Pardon me, but don't you live in Blarney Lane?'

'No,' she said, 'I'm from Gunpowder Lane if you know where that is.'

'Ah sure I do,' he said, 'sure I do.'

The picture being more valuable took a lot of selling but eventually it was purchased by a young woman who in response to the same type of devious questioning said she was from the Rock Steps. The purchaser of St Anthony was from Pouladuff. 'A long way off... a long way off,' said The Saint as he parted with the last of his treasures. Hobbling homewards he repeated his lesson over and over again: The Angel in Gunpowder Lane, Holy Mother in a house on the Rock Steps, St Anthony in Pouladuff.

Next day he paid the rent for Mrs Phelan and straightaway began to save his pennies so that one day he could buy back his treasures. He sadly missed them. Because of the blank spaces the room looked upset and unfurnished, the worst gap of all being the huge space of clean wallpaper where the picture had hung. But being a saint as well as a child his savings refused to mount up. How could he pass a blind man's hand stretched out to the callous passers-by or a hungry looking child staring in at a shop window? Again and again he had to start anew.

Then as the anniversary of the sale approached his savings began to mount again and soon he had enough to buy back his treasures. When the day arrived he rose early and left the house. He came in at one o'clock and called to the lady he had befriended, 'Mrs Mehigan, I have one of them, the angel.' At five he passed up again, 'Mrs Mehigan, I've another, St Anthony!' He went out again and when he hadn't returned Mrs Mehigan concluded that he had failed to get the last one. Towards midnight she heard him struggling up the stairs once more, falling from side to side and sometimes missing steps.

The next morning when he didn't appear the bed-ridden Mrs Mehigan asked Mrs Phelan to knock at his door. Getting no response she went back to Mrs Mehigan. She went up again and there was no answer. Mrs Mehigan told her to go for the priest. When they entered the room, they found The Saint sitting on the floor, an unfinished bowl of bread and milk between his legs. Opposite his now cold eyes was his beloved Madonna, it stood propped against the edge of the bed. Guarding it on the right was St Anthony, on the left the chinaware angel, its font full of holy water. The candle that had lighted his treasures for him had burnt out. Mrs Phelan says that when she entered the room there was the smell of beautiful flowers. Mrs Mehigan says she heard far-away singing in the dead of night. In any case it is pleasant to think how sweet the old man's thoughts must have been as his eyes began to close for ever. No far away music or newly-gathered flowers could be sweeter.

The following verses were given to me by my good friend Travers. They are a fitting eulogy of *agape!*

Faith looks out at a drowning man
And faith had not a doubt
But that some hand would reach and pull
The struggling fellow out

Hope looked out at the self-same man
And hope had not a frown
For she was sure as sure can be
The man would never drown

Love looked out at the drowning man
And love had faith and hope
But love had more, her hand was swift
She threw the man a rope.

10

In Praise of Women

Helmer says to Nora: 'Before anything else you are a woman and a mother.'
Nora answers: 'I don't believe that anymore. I believe that I am in the very first place a human being, just like you.'
He: 'You are talking like a child, you don't understand anything of the society in which you live.'
She: 'That is true. I don't understand it. But from now on I will go on to try to discover who is right, society or I'.

HENRIK IBSEN, *A Doll's House* 1879

A school girl once wrote an essay on why there were more women in the world then men. 'God made Adam first,' she wrote, 'When he had finished, he looked at him and said, "I think I'll try again. I'm sure I could do better than that." So then he made Eve. And God liked Eve so much better than Adam that he has been making more women than men ever since!'

The self-assurance of this young feminist stands out against the prevailing attitude to women over the centuries. 'There is no doubt,' writes John Stott, 'that in many cultures women have habitually been despised and demeaned by men. They have often been regarded as mere playthings and sex-objects, as brainless simpletons incapable of engaging in rational discussion. Their gifts have been unappreciated, their personality smothered, their freedom curtailed and their service in some areas exploited, in others refused.'

In a chat show on television a Jewish mayor admitted that

in his morning prayer he gave thanks that God had not made him a Gentile, a slave or a woman! By way of defence he claimed that this form of morning prayer was enshrined in the *Talmud*. Aristotle held that women's inferiority was based on the belief that women were conceived either when the sperm were weak or when the south wind was blowing in the wrong direction! And, wait for it, Thomas Aquinas whose admiration for the Greek philosopher was unbounded contended that the latter point was a matter of natural law! Tertullian, one of the great theologians of the early Church influenced more by Greek and Jewish sources than by the Scriptures vented his feelings towards woman in these terms, 'You are the devil's gateway; you are the unsealer of that forbidden tree; you are the first deserter of the divine law; you are she who persuaded him whom the devil was not valiant enough to attack. You destroyed so easily God's image, man. On account of your action even the Son of God had to die.'

One final example of early male chauvinism this time from Ireland. Tradition has it that when the monks of Inishmurray, being the only inhabitants on that island, requested permission to keep a cow there, St Colmcille refused on the grounds that 'an áit a bhíonn bó, bíonn bean, agus an áit a bhíonn bean bíonn buaireamh' (where there is a cow there is a woman and where there is a woman there is mischief). It was a social taboo at the time for a man to milk a cow. The poor monks had to carry on without their cow.

The Irish however soon redeemed themselves because St Brigid and St Patrick (in that order) are cited in the seventh century *Liber Angelorum* as the twin pillars of the door of heaven in Ireland, the inference being that one was as powerful as the other. Brigid herself was a dynamic figure. She was given the task of organising the Church in the province of Leinster; she headed two religious communities, one male, the other female. Once she was summoned to the death-bed of a pagan chieftain. He asked her to tell him about her God so Brigid took two strands from the floor of reeds,

twisted then into the shape of a cross and holding it before
the chief told him the story of Christ's redeeming love. He
died clasping the cross shortly after Brigid had baptised him.
This cross is now the identification symbol of Ireland's
national television station.

What was Christ's attitude to women? As Christians we
must believe that in the Incarnation God took human form in
the person of Jesus Christ. He is both true God and true man.
When he became man he took his entire and complete
human nature from a woman, Mary his mother. Woman
then was used by God in a unique way. She is mankind's sole
contribution to his act of redemptive love.

How did Christ treat women? The Scriptures tell us that in
addition to the apostles who were all men he was accompanied in his travels by a group of women who provided for
him out of their means.

The women in his life were extraordinary by any stan-
dards. There was the busy Martha and the wild Mary; there
was the pushy mother of James and John who asked for
much and received nothing and the weeping widow of Nain
who asked for nothing and received much. There was Peter's
mother-in-law whom he cured and who lost no time in
getting back to work; there was Mary Magdalene whom he
restored to grace and the young daughter of Jairus whom he
restored to life. When the time came for the supreme revelation that he was the Messiah the first to receive it was not a
theologian who might have argued with him but the woman
at the well who simply believed in him. Then there were the
women of Good Friday, the weeping women of Jerusalem,
the fearless Veronica and the three Marys at the foot of the
cross.

It goes without saying that the women in his life were completely and utterly faithful to him. We read with sorrow of
the shouting failure of Peter, of the treachery of Judas, of the
flight of the rest of the apostles, but never once do we read of
a woman who deserted him. And see how he rewarded their
fidelity. The Resurrection came for the women before it came

for the fickle and cowardly men. Mary Magdalene was the first fruit of the Resurrection. She was the first to see the Risen Christ. Mary, his mother was the first human body after his own to be taken up in glory. These are the two women who above all their kind bore witness to the love of Christ for women and the love of women for Christ.

Much has been said and written about Paul's teaching on male headship. This however was conditioned by the Greek and Jewish cultures in which he lived. If Paul told wives to submit to their husbands he also told slaves to submit to their masters. Slaves have long since been liberated so isn't it high time that women were liberated too? Personally, I feel that Paul spoke the decisive words about women's equality and liberation in Galatians 3:28, namely that from now on 'there is no difference between... men and women'. You have Paul the apostle of Christian liberty and Paul the Jewish rabbi. You take your pick. I prefer the former.

The vivid biblical images of wind, earthquake and fire appropriately describe the debate in Anglican and more liberal Catholic circles on the ordination of women. The wind is personified by the heated and bad-tempered debates in the media; the earthquake by modern feminism with its distrust, and depising of men, a feminism which has little interest in priesting as such and which berates the Church demanding the removal of male dominance and superiority.

But one element in the story is missing, a still small voice, the voice of the ordinary woman who Sunday after Sunday prays quietly in the local church. How can her voice be heard? Margaret Hood is a wife, a mother and until recently a sister in a London teaching hospital. In a feature in *The Times* (18 January 1986) she makes a plea for what she calls Christian feminism. It is a plea to woman to consider her unique bond with God through the Incarnation. Woman did not need the priesthood because she was to be used by God in the Incarnation; her unique relationship with creation through motherhood and for those women who either voluntarily give up or who are denied the ultimate fulfilment of their womanhood, the offering back to God of their pain and loss and deprivation. 'I firmly believe,' she concludes, 'that this Christian feminism is a fundamental idea that lies behind the debate about the ordination of woman. They are the most important reasons why I as a woman can never accept a woman as priest.'

In our homilies we might just occasionally turn to the women and say a few words that are meant just for them. After all they are the best attenders. You rarely see them crowding around the door and were it not for them there would be little point in having week-day masses. By and large they are the more religious of the two sexes. Some would deny this, pointing to the fact that the overwhelming majority of canonised saints are men. True, but then in whose hands is the canonisation process?

Father Patrick J. Peyton the great crusader for the family rosary tells the remarkable story of the three women in his life. One of thirteen children he remembers how the entire family used pray the daily rosary in front of the kitchen fire. He recalls the smell of home-made bread and draws an analogy between it and the call to priesthood which came to himself and his brother Tom. It was home-made because love-made. In the seminary Pat fell victim to a severe case of tuberculosis. He was on the brink of death when the doctors noticed a sudden and inexplicable improvement leading to a complete healing within a week. To this day Father Pat is convinced that Mary saved him. Later he discovered that his mother and sister had prayed that his suffering be transferred to them so that he could continue his course and become a priest. Two days before he left hospital his mother died and shortly before the brothers were ordained the sister also died. After her death Pat was leafing through her prayer book when he found a prayer in her own handwriting composed when he was in hospital. She had offered her life to God instead of his. I heard Pat Peyton tell this story at one of his family prayer rallies to a crowd of 25,000 and his conclusion? He owed his priesthood to the love of three women, Mary, his mother, and his sister. Pat is now approaching four score years but his crusade across the world goes on unabated... in praise of women.

A priest was making his daily holy hour in the church when he was disturbed by a sudden commotion at the shrine of Our Lady. An irate mother was giving a tongue lashing to her child much to the annoyance of the priest. As she came down the church dragging the protesting child after her he decided to confront her. He reminded her that this was a house of prayer not a stage for domestic conflicts. The woman stopped in her tracks turned to him and said, 'Father, I was so absorbed in the situation of my child almost setting fire to himself and the church into the bargain through fooling about with lighted candles that I did not notice your presence. Now, while you were on your knees you were absorbed in someone far more precious than my child. How is it then that you noticed me?'

An old lady would sit for hours in the church rapt in prayer, her lips motionless. One day a priest asked her what God talked to her about.
'God doesn't talk. He just listens,' was her reply.
'Well then what do you talk to him about?'
'I don't talk either. I just listen.'
I talk, you listen; you talk, I listen; Neither of us talks, we both listen: Contemplation.

A priest noticed a woman sitting in an empty church, her head in her hands. She was still there when he left an hour later. When he returned to the church later still he found her in the same place. Judging her to be a soul in distress he went to her and said, 'Is there any way I can be of help?'
'No, thank you, Father!' she said, 'I've been getting all the help I need!'
She returned her head to her hands and as the priest left he

heard her whisper ' . . . and now Lord what were we talking about when we were interrupted?'

It is the lot of every mother to suffer and to worry over erring children. Rebecca was no exception. A devout Jewish wife and mother she was venerated by her husband and six daughters as a saint and the principal cause of all the blessings they had received from God. When she died there was rejoicing amongst the angels and saints as they prepared a tumultuous welcome for her. However, throughout the festivities Rebecca looked sad and withdrawn. The Lord came to her and spoke kindly, 'why are you so sad Rebecca? Rejoice and be glad you are receiving your just reward for being such a virtuous wife and mother.'

'Ah, Lord,' Rebecca replied, 'I can never be happy thinking of my only son. Did you know that he abandoned the faith of our fathers, and became a Christian?'

'Rebecca dear,' said the Lord, 'I know exactly how you feel. Did you know that I too had an only son and he did the same thing?'

There is a lovely story in the Jewish *Talmud* on the value of a good wife. It caught the imagination of the poet Samuel T. Coleridge who translated it into English. It tells of a virtuous wife whose husband was the celebrated teacher Rabbi Meir. Once he was away from home teaching in various schools and synagogues and during his absence his two young sons died. His wife took them to her bed-chamber, laid them upon the marriage bed and spread a white covering over their bodies. That evening Rabbi Meir came home and asked for his sons so that he might give them his blessing. 'They will not be far off,' she said as she placed his evening meal before him.

When he had eaten she addressed him, 'Husband dear, I would like to put a question to you!'

'Ask it, then, my love!' he replied.

'A short time ago a person entrusted some jewels to my

safe-keeping and now he demands them again. Should I give them back again?'

'There's no need to ask such a question,' said Rabbi Meir, 'don't you know that you should restore to everyone his own?'

'Come with me, then,' she said leading him to the bedroom. She took off the white cloth covering the bodies of their sons.

United in grief they threw their arms around each other and wept bitterly. At length she took her husband by the hand and said, 'Rabbi, did you not teach me that we must not be reluctant to restore that which was entrusted to our keeping? See, the Lord gave, the Lord has taken away, and blessed be the name of the Lord!'

'Blessed be the name of the Lord!' echoed Rabbi Meir, 'and blessed be his name for your sake too, for well it is written, 'he that found a virtuous wife has a greater treasure than costly pearls. She opens her mouth with wisdom, and on her tongue is the instruction of kindness.'

11

All the Lonely People

*When stories are shared, you discover that your longings are
universal longings, that you are not lonely and isolated. You belong.
That is part of the beauty of stories.*

F. SCOTT FITZGERALD

*All the Lonely People
Where do They all Come From?*

This is the haunting refrain of a Beatles' song from the
1960s. The ballad of 'Eleanor Rigby' is about a lonely priest
and a lonely spinster. Like a lot of modern pop music it
contains a philosophy of reflection on the meaning of life.
Here the theme is loneliness. The priest Father Mackenzie
alone in his room is 'writing the words of a sermon no one
will hear'. And then those poignant words:

*No-one comes near
Darning his socks at night when nobody's there*

The priest is alone in his loneliness.
If Father Mackenzie were to write his sermon on loneliness
it would be safe to bet that quite a few of his congregation
would hear because he would be touching a life experience
common to everyone. 'Most people go through life in a coffin
of loneliness,' said one of the interviewers on a recent television programme. He was stating something that should be
obvious to every preacher. Loneliness is one of the diseases
of modern society.

In the course of his pastoral work, visiting homes, hospitals, and particulary geriatric institutions the priest is constantly meeting the lonely people. As we walk through the wards of an old people's home do we ever pause to think that in each bed there is a story to tell if only we have time to spare and ears to hear? Take for instance the story of Elizabeth.

Elizabeth was in a small room at the end of a long dusky corridor in an old people's home. She was the last on my round of communion calls, and sad to relate my visits to her were for a long time routine and perfunctory. Then one evening as I was about to leave I noticed a French book on her bed-side locker.

'So you speak French?' I ventured.

'Yes father,' she replied, 'I spent some time in France.'

Then she told me her story. After a few years in France she moved to Canada where her proficiency in French secured rapid promotion for her in the civil service. Eventually she became secretary to a cabinet minister. One of her duties was to manage state banquets and receptions for visiting dignitaries. She married and life became a constant round of glittering social functions. Then her husband died. There were no children so she had her first experience of loneliness. Her home became just four walls in an alien city in an alien land.

She returned to Ireland and set up home again. Peggy, her favourite niece, came to live with her. After a few months Peggy died of cancer and Elizabeth was alone again. Being a 'blow-in' as newcomers are tagged by the long established members of our community she had few callers, door bell and telephone were silent. For the third time in as many months she packed her belongings once more and took herself off to a nursing home where she was to spend the remainder of her days alone with her memories. It was a drab November evening. The four walls of the tiny room seemed to close in on her. As I rose to leave her parting words were, 'Thank you for taking time to listen.'

Michael Quoist in *The Prayer of a Priest on Sunday Night* could be echoing the thoughts of Father Mackenzie. He speaks of the feelings of loneliness which befall a celibate priest and he protests angrily against the amount of love he is expected to give others in, 'Lord, why did you tell me to love?'

There are two aspects of loneliness which we might consider in our preaching and counselling, one is a temptation, the other an invitation.

The temptation consists in the feeling that I am alone, isolated and cut off from the rest of the world. As the Beatles' song reminds us there are so many lonely people and so many varieties of the loneliness they experience. We were never intended to live in isolation. We need to belong. We were designed to live in contact and relationship with other people; being cut off from other people is not just a matter of being separated from then by walls or distance. You can live in the midst of bustling activity surrounded by people and yet be desperately lonely.

Paul Mercier the Irish playwright has written a powerful drama which he calls *Home*. It describes the loneliness of the country boy from the Irish midlands who comes to Dublin in search of work and finds himself in a bed-sitter. Around him like a frame is a three-tiered set which portrays the tensions and goings-on of flatland – a couple fighting over a vacuum cleaner, others disputing access to a communal loo and centre stage our hero missing the familiar surroundings of home – the hill, the glen, the windows with the familiar scene, isolated from the world as if he were in the solitary confinement of a prison cell.

Strange isn't it that if you build a street vertically instead of horizontally you do something to the people who live in it. Instead of feeling that you belong you feel desperately isolated. You seldom if ever meet your neighbours and could be ill, or even dead for weeks without anyone knowing it. The new face of alienation in the secular city – lonely in the crowd!

There was a man who was so lonely and isolated from his fellow humans that he yearned for the human touch, the clasp of a hand in friendship, the warm embrace of a woman, the friendly pat on the back, but there was no one to touch him or make him feel wanted and appreciated. In desperation he decided to spend the last of his money but not on food. Food would not help, it does not make contact. He did not spend it on drink because to drink alone would be just going down a blind alley in his loneliness. So he spent his last money on a hairdressers, so that he would be touched and cared for by another person if only for a few minutes.

Loneliness is also an invitation, with an RSVP attached. All of us can point to people living on their own who are not lonely. It is not just that they are happy by nature but rather that they have found a new relationship with an unseen companion. Loneliness whether it be caused by bereavement, disappointment or alienation creates a vacuum in my life which can only be filled by someone who is really understanding and sympathetic and who knows me better than I know myself. Such a friend is my greatest need if my trouble is loneliness. And there is such a friend knocking at the door of the human heart.

A priest went to visit a man who had lost his wife. They had lived together for years after the fledglings had flown the nest to make lives of their own. The priest's mission was one of comfort and consolation but he went away the beneficiary of the visit. When he asked if the man minded being on his own the reply he received was, 'Where there's one of us now. . . there will always be three of us. . . herself and myself and Him!'

This sense of God's presence and the need to grow into an ever-deepening relationship with him by accepting him into my life as Lord and Saviour is the RSVP to the invitation. Leave an empty chair by your bed for him. Leave a chair by the fire for him. Learn to talk to him, to reflect on him, to listen to him. Listen to his voice in the pages of Scripture; be his voice and hands and feet to bring comfort and consolation to others in your predicament who may be housebound. Our loneliness is often swallowed up by dispelling that of others.

A. Price Hughes in his book *A Warrior on Wines* wrote:

If I should die and leave you here awhile
Be not like others sore undone who keep
Lone vigils by the silent dust and weep;
For my sake, turn to life again and smile,
Nerving thy heart and trembling hand to do
something to comfort weaker hearts than thine
And I, perchance, may therein comfort you.

In this way we turn our sacrifice of loneliness into service.

12

Filling the Emptiness

On the eve of Christmas and the Epiphany it is the Irish custom to put a lighted candle in the window, put down a fire, sweep the hearth, leave food and drink on the table and go off to bed. It is our way of saying 'Fáilte' to the Holy Family – you are welcome to our house.

ARCHBISHOP JOSEPH CASSIDY

'Write something about Christmas!' The call was from London and it was a *cri du coeur*. Paul was dead, and for Rita Christmas would never be the same again. The emptiness in her voice reflected the emptiness in her life, because Paul was too young to die. Together they had built up a successful business, seen their family settled and had bought for themselves a dream house back in Ireland where they planned to enjoy life together in early retirement. And then Paul died. He was not yet fifty years old. Life for Rita had suddenly become empty.

It is really hard to know why God chose Bethlehem. It had nothing to offer. It was not the sort of place where people would stop over on their journey. It was a lonely place. It was here that Ruth, the girl from Moab, sick for home, 'stood in tears amid the alien corn'. True, her great grandson David would bring glory to Bethlehem but that was a millennium ago. Now Bethlehem was an empty village on the road to nowhere. That is the point. Because it was insignificant,

because it was empty, God was able to fill it. Speaking
through the prophet Micah, 'Bethlehem Ephrathah, you are
one of the smallest towns in Judah, but out of you I will bring
a Ruler for Israel' (Mic 5:2).

In the liturgy leading up to Christmas two women figure
prominently, Mary and Elizabeth. Both were empty, Elizabeth was sterile and Mary was a virgin. In the midst of such
emptiness both conceive, not by their own power or that of
their husbands but with God's power. He filled their emptiness, Elizabeth's with John the Baptist, Mary's with Jesus.

Christmas is a time when many of us, like Rita, make
contact with our emptiness. A child leaves home, a loved one
dies, we are confronted by the empty chair, the empty space
and left with a feeling of emptiness. Into this emptiness God
comes, he comes to fill us up. 'Behold I stand at the door and
knock'. . . the door is the human heart. He comes in so many
ways to fill our emptiness, a word of comfort, a reconciliation, the rediscovery of a lost friendship; he comes to us in
word and sacrament if only we would listen to his voice and
let him in.

The trouble is that so often we are too busy filling ourselves that there is no room to let God in, there is no room in
the inn. The pre-Christmas slogan is '...so many shopping
days left'. Our time and our lives are so filled with shopping,
running here and there, planning, decorating, worrying and
we are so exhausted by Christmas that the slogan now
becomes: 'How did you get over the Christmas?'

There is no room for God in all of this. God cannot get into
fulness, only into emptiness like the emptiness of Bethlehem,
the emptiness of Mary, the emptiness of Elizabeth. Strange
isn't it, that when Bethlehem was filled with the fulness of
God on that first Christmas the first to get the message were
the shepherds and the wise men.

The shepherds watching their flocks by night found God
in silence and emptiness; the wise men sensitive to the

emptiness of human knowledge saw a star and using their God-given talents were led to the one who created the stars. Simeon too got the message. He studied the sacred writings not as an exegete but in search of the Christ and found him in that never-to-be forgotten encounter in the Temple.

It is interesting to note the types that missed out. There was no room in the inn. The inn-keeper who could have written himself into history was a busy man. He had to keep his guests happy and, after all, that was his livelihood. How was he to know who that young couple were who came knocking on his door that night? The lines of cars outside our modern-day inns before and after the first Mass of Christmas recall the inn of Bethlehem, only in those days it was horses that were tied up outside. Horse-power was much safer when the horse had it. Besides, the horse was never invited in!

The men of violence missed out too. Herod saw the child as a threat and his determination to murder him made him insensitive to the death of so many others. Even at his birth Christ met with human hatred and children were the first to suffer for his sake. Had Herod found room for him he would have reigned securely here and hereafter.

A heroic story of God filling emptiness, this time the emptiness of a prison cell in Red China, is told by Father Patrick Reilly, a Columban missionary in *The Far East*, December 1988. For fourteen months he had been in solitary confinement. There was no bed to lie on, he was forced to sit in the one position for sixteen hours every day and was allowed nothing to read not even a letter from home. His only visitors were his guards and interrogators. Twice a day the cell door opened to admit a meagre ration of rice and a tiny bowl of vegetables. He takes up the story: 'I saw my body withering away. One day they weighed me. I was astonished when I realised that I had gone from twelve to less than six and a half stone. . . A few times I tried to stand upright, and collapsed. I thought I was going to die. My wish

was to say just one more Mass before I died. But locked away
how could I. It would need a miracle.'

Then one day to his surprise he was given steamed bread
instead of the usual rice. All he needed now was wine to have
the essentials for celebrating Mass. The words of Mary at last
flashed into his mind: 'Son they have no wine!' He prayed to
our Lady for the impossible. As his health deteriorated he
was examined by the prison doctor who suggested that he be
given fruit. When he was asked what fruit he would like he
asked for grapes.

A bunch of grapes was handed into his cell that evening.
He tore the cuffs from the sleeves of the shirt he was wearing
when arrested, washed them in his ration of drinking water,
made a little bag of one cuff and put some of the grapes into
it. He squeezed the juice from them gathering it in his rice
bowl. The juice was poured into a little bottle which he had
kept concealed. He corked the bottle and hid it.

A few days later the cork popped from the bottle. The juice
had fermented; it was now wine. He could say Mass. Now
let's hear him describe his Miracle Mass: 'not being allowed
to move in the cell, and being constantly under guard, I had
to be very careful. I washed a small portion of the cell floor
which would serve as an altar. Then I waited. Towards the
evening I heard the guard on duty scolding another prisoner.
I knew by the tone of his voice that he was going to spend at
least ten minutes questioning him. This was my opportunity.
I got up and spread the other cuff of the shirt sleeve on the
section of the ground which I had washed.

'I placed the piece of bread on it. I put some wine into the
little mug which normally held my vegetable ration. Dressed
only in my shirt and pants, and barefooted, I knelt down. I
took the bread and offered it up to God whispering the
beautiful offertory prayer: "Accept, O Holy Father, Almighty
and Eternal God, this Immaculate Host which I, thy unwor-
thy servant offer unto Thee, my living and true God, for my
innumerable sins, offences and negligences, and for all here
present and also for all faithful Christians, both living and

dead, that it may profit my own and their salvation unto life everlasting. Amen."

'Then I took the little mug with wine, and whispered: "We offer unto Thee, O God, the chalice of salvation." I hurried to the Consecration. Again I took the bread in my hands and began: "Who the day before he suffered took bread into His Holy and Venerable Hands... saying: "This Is My Body." Then I took the mug, saying: "This Is My Blood".

'Jesus Christ was really present with me in that cell. All other visitors had been prevented from coming near me, because of many locked doors. But they could not stop the King of Kings. It had been a long fourteen months without Mass, but I could not delay, I could not savour the moment. I omitted the rest of the Mass up to the Communion.

'Having consumed both species, I hurriedly purified the little mug, washed the piece of linen which served as an altar cloth, and sat down. All was over in a few minutes. The guard was still scolding the other prisoner.

'Imagine the joy of receiving this Visitor into my cell. I had only the floor and the cuff of my shirt on which to lay His Sacred Body. I thought of the first Christmas night when He was willing to be wrapped by Mary in swaddling clothes and laid in a manger. Our God is a humble God and He comes to us in all circumstances and conditions.

'That evening was all too short for me to spend in thanking Him. He was the only kind visitor in fourteen months, and He had answered my prayer to be able to say another Mass before I died. Not once, but twelve times was I able to say Mass before the wine ran short.'

Father Patrick Reilly survived his ordeal in China. Eventually he was set free but expelled from the country. He is now working in a parish in his native Ireland.

An old Russian folktale tells of Befana the housewife who was busy cleaning her windows when the wise men passed by on their way to Bethlehem. They told her about the Christ-child, showed her their gifts and invited her to come along

with them. She said she would and she would bring with her
a pillow for the child's head and a robe to warm his sleep but
first she had to attend to her household chores, dusting and
cleaning and polishing. Then she set out with her gifts
hoping to catch up with the wise men, but she failed to find
them, neither did she find the place where the Christ-child
lay. According to the legend she is still searching, at least that
is how the story goes in a little ditty by an unknown author.

> And still she wanders at Christmastide
> Houseless, whose house was all her pride,
> Whose heart was tardy, whose gifts were late,
> Wanders and knocks at every gate,
> Crying, 'Good people, the bells begin;
> Put off your toiling and let love in'.

13

Did Jesus Laugh?

Two books he read with great affection
The Gospels and a joke collection
And sang hosannas set to fiddles
And fed the sick on soup and riddles
So when the grave rebuke the merry
Let them remember Philip Neri
(1515 to 95)
Who was the merriest man alive
Then dying at eighty or a bit
Became a saint by holy wit.

ANON

'Did Jesus ever laugh?' I once put this question to Dom Eugene Boylan the Cistercian Abbot and noted spiritual writer.

'Of course he did,' came the reply, 'laughter is part and parcel of every normal man's personality!'

'Strange then, isn't it,' I countered, 'that the Scriptures record every human emotion in Christ except laughter. We read that he wept, that he was weary, that he experienced anger, sorrow, depression, but never once does the good book say that he laughed.'

Eugene was silent for a moment then fixing me with that searching gaze of his said, 'Have it your own way but that's not the person I pray to.' He continued to muse and as if expressing his thoughts aloud said, 'How in God's name could he have told Zacchaeus to get down out that tree without a smile? How could he have given that twelve year old girl back to her parents without a smile on his lips? How could he have called the unstable Peter, "Rocky", without a grin? Of course he laughed,' he concluded, 'so did his followers. Can't you imagine that bunch of clerics going around together for three years without cracking a joke? And so should we laugh. There's enough sadness and tears in life and after all isn't joy one of the sure indicators of the presence of his Spirit in our lives?'

There's an ancient Russian Orthodox tradition where people come together to tell jokes and funny stories on the day after Easter. The custom has its origin in the great cosmic joke of Christ's victory over death and Satan. When Jesus breathed his last on the afternoon of Good Friday the sky darkened and it seemed as if the powers of evil were in control and Satan had the last word. Then came Easter and Resurrection and the world laughed at Satan's comeuppance.

'This attitude passed into the mediaeval concept of *hilaritas*,' writes William Bausch, 'which did not mean mindless giggling but, that even at the moment of disaster one may wink because he or she knows that there is a God.' This is borne out by Montalembert in *Monks of the West* where he points out that the Church has always sought certain qualities of its clergy – simplicity, benignity and... HILARITY!

And what about the homilist? Dare he be funny? 'By God, he'd better,' says William Burghardt, 'for his own salvation and for the redemption of his congregation!' A story which provokes a ripple of laughter in the pews can be a welcome antidote provided of course that it is relevant to the message. To tell a funny story because it is a funny story is to trivialise preaching.

In our seminary days we had to endure at least four sermons by students each week, invariably gleaned from dusty old commentaries and as a result excessively serious and soporific. We suffered through them week after week until one evening when an aspiring Fulton Sheen decided to capture our attention with a sequence of funny stories. He succeeded. We closed our books and gave vent to gales of laughter as the preacher bombarded us with his wit and humour. The professor of homiletics sat listening at the back of the chapel and for the benefit of us all delivered his critique in a few cryptic sentences. 'The preacher,' he said, 'apart from a few primitive crudities of speech has good delivery and is to be commended on establishing instant rapport with his congregation. As for the content of his homily... I would suggest to him that in future and particularly when he is on the mission that he would apply himself more to feeding the sheep then to amusing the goats.'

One of the great masters of the craft of humorous illustration is Michael Cleary of Dublin. A preacher in great demand he gets the rapt attention of his people as he breaks the bread of the word with them and then has them rollicking in the pews with his inimitable shafts of humour.

The trouble is, as William Burghardt rightly points out, many if not most Catholic congregations are not ready for homiletic humour and the reason for this is that we priests have not led them to expect it in the pulpit. As a consequence the funny story often falls flat and the more subtle humour tends to get lost. To revert to the *hilarity* of Easter, as risen Christians we must be creatures of joy and laughter like the hero of Eugene O' Neill's play *Lazarus Laughed* who in the new found joy of living cries out to the audience:

> Laugh with me
> Death is dead
> Fear is no more
> There is only life!
> There is only laughter

Lena, my housekeeper, is a firm believer in the religious dimension of humour. Every week she troops off to a Novena in Holy Cross Abbey and on her return regales me with her commentary on the homily. 'He told a funny story,' she says, and then after the re-telling, 'Wasn't that a good one?' adding philosophically 'sure there's nothing like a laugh!'

A remark like that gives a proper sense of proportion. Richard Harries, a well-known religious broadcaster on Radio 4, holds that religion needs to be joked about more than anything in the world. 'Only God is to be taken with unreserved seriousness but... our ideas of God and the things of religion often go badly wrong here, and so in order to keep itself from blasphemy religion needs plenty of jokes.' As an example he gives one gleaned from *Private Eye:*

A trendy parson was in the pulpit saying, 'Of course God isn't an old man with a long white beard in the sky' and above him was an-old-man-with-a-white-beard-type-of-God looking down and saying, 'How does he know?'

This reminds me of the story of a young curate who hurried to his parish priest saying 'There's an old man with a long white beard at the back of the church who says he is God, what shall I do?'

'Go and keep an eye on him,' said the pastor, 'and try and look busy!'

Children love funny stories. They can be more perceptive than a lot of us think. Take my young friend Louise. She has just turned five and recently she caused consternation in the church as the people, including her parents, were making their thanksgiving after Communion. She stood on the seat and pointed an accusing finger at the celebrant who was carrying out the ablutions, 'Look at him mummy,' she exclaimed aloud, 'look at him up there drinking whiskey himself.' The celebrant had earlier delivered a homily on temperance! 'Blessed are the ears. . . !'

Then there was the little girl who showed a touching concern for God in her night-prayer, 'Please bless and take care of mammy and daddy and my little brother Tommy, and please God, do take care of yourself, because if anything happens to you, we're sunk!'

And the little boy in a similar situation, 'Please God,' he

shouted, 'get me a bicycle for my birthday.'

'Keep your voice down Tommy,' his mother called, 'God is not deaf.'

'I know,' Tommy called back, 'but Granpa is next door, and he is deaf.'

A little boy in boarding school wrote to his parents: 'Dear mum and dad. Last week the bishop came for Confirmation. I had a good view of him from where I sat in the chapel and now I know what a crook really looks like.'

Bishops, like all establishment figures, have always been a subject for humour. There is a classic tale of Archbishop Trench of Dublin. As he reached the biblical age of three score and ten he became obsessed with the fear of sudden and crippling paralysis. On one occasion he was invited out to dine and throughout the meal he could be heard muttering to himself, 'My God, it has come at last... so it's come at last... total insensibility in the right limb.' As coffee was served the lady beside him turned and said, 'Your Grace, it may be of some comfort and relief to you to know that during the whole of the meal it has been my leg that you have been pinching!'

An eminent ecclesiastic reduced to two the basic qualifications required for the office of bishop – to suffer fools gladly and to answer letters by return of post. Archbishop Curley of Baltimore had considerable difficulty in conforming to the first. On one occasion during a cathedral ceremony a rather nervous chaplain placed the mitre on the prelate's head back to front. Curley glared at him through the flaps and growled, 'Now turn around and let the people see what a fool you are.' The priest chastened by the experience removed the mitre and as he hesitantly faced the ordeal for the second time Curley snapped, 'Put it on! Put it on!' whereupon the flustered chaplain place the mitre on his own head! Later in the more relaxed atmosphere of the sacristy the Archbishop gently chided his victim who summoned up the courage to respond, 'Your grace, I'm afraid you do not suffer fools gladly,' to which Curley replied with the glimmer of a smile 'Perhaps not, but I do *suffer* them!'

Examples of episcopal wit and humour abound. When Archbishop Mannix of Melbourne was admonished by an Apostlic Delegate for 'improvident' spending on his cathedral he delivered the now famous *coup de grâce*. 'The criticism voiced by your Excellency lacks originality. Similar sentiments have been expressed at another time in another place by another ecclesiastic in a high place, in the words "Wherefore this waste"!'

It was a bishop of another persuasion, Dr Archibald Spooner, who gave the English language one of its most colourful figures of speech. A classic spoonerism: meeting a man who had studied under him at Oxford and who asked if Spooner remembered him got this reply 'I remember your name quite well, but I must admit that I've completely forgotten your face!'

Then there was the bishop who arrived at the cathedral door for his enthronement. Having given the customary three knocks and received no reply he was about to repeat the ritual when the door opened to reveal a rather decrepit dean, archdeacon and chapter of canons waiting to greet him. As the procession turned to make its arthritic way to the sanctuary the new prelate out of earshot whispered to his chaplain, 'The see gives up its dead!'

The shortest story in this category is about the bishop who lamented, 'Everywhere Christ went there was a revolution, everywhere I go they serve cups of tea!'

Now to the priests! The pulpit has always provided a forum for priests' wit and idiosyncrasies. The classic story of clerical humility is the one about the curate's egg. The curate is having breakfast with the bishop who remarks, 'I'm afraid you've got a bad egg, Father Jones!' to which the curate replies, 'Oh no, my Lord, I assure you! Parts of it are quite excellent!'

There's a story about a parish priest on pastoral visitation. He rang one door-bell and when he got no response, although he could hear music playing inside he left his visiting card having written on the back 'Revelation 3.20' (Listen! I stand at the door and knock; if anyone hears my voice and opens the door, I will come into his house'). As he greeted his parishioners the following Sunday a lady handed him an envelope and hurried into the church.

The message was brief. It simply read: Genesis 3:10. He looked it up and read, 'I heard you in the garden; I was afraid and hid from you, because I was naked.'

There was the priest preaching in a mental hospital and he began his homily with 'Why are we all here?'

A voice came from the pews, 'Because we're not all there!'

And the young priest carried away on a wave of emotion who exhorted his congregation not to leave the church without, 'Pure hearts, clean hearts, loving hearts and sweethearts!'

Another preacher proclaimed, 'The readings this morning have an important message for all here, young and old, rich and poor, high and low, for you old man with your hoary head, 'and spying a comely rosy complexioned young lady in the front pews,' he concluded, 'and for you young maiden with your blooming cheek!'

The most irritating interruption to any homily is a crying baby. On one occasion one started up as a preacher approached the ambo. He decided to change the subject of the homily and began as follows: 'My homily this morning is about good resolutions; but good resolutions aren't of much use unless they are what that baby must be – carried out!'

People themselves provide a continuous source of apt and imaginative illustrations. A priest travelling on a bus found himself sitting beside a hippie. He noticed that the hippie had only one shoe and remarked, 'I see you lost a shoe.'

'No man,' came the reply, 'I found one.'

Martin, like Zacchaeus, was small of stature. He fell in love with a very tall girl. They began to meet on a regular basis and every evening Martin would walk her home. He longed to kiss her but was too shy to ask. One evening he summoned up the courage and asked if he might kiss her. She agreed but the problem was how to reach her. They were passing an abandoned blacksmith's forge so Martin stood on the anvil which provided him with the required height and received his kiss. They walked on for the best part of an hour and Martin once more ventured, 'Could I trouble you for another kiss, please?'

'No,' came the reply, 'You've had your quota for this evening.'

'Blast it,' said Martin 'then why didn't you stop me from carrying this bloody anvil?'

As we began, so let us finish this section with a lovely story about St Philip Neri. When he was an old man, a young priest came to him and asked him about the stages he had passed through in his quest for holiness. 'First, I found myself in the Land of Action,' said Philip, 'the day wasn't long enough to do all the things I wanted to do. Then God came to me and took me by the hand and led me into the Land of Sorrow. There I experienced the purifying effect of suffering and found myself in a new relationship with the divine. This led me into the Land of Love where the last traces of self disappeared. This brought me to the Land of Silence where I discovered contemplation.'

'And that was the end of your journey?'

'No,' said Philip. 'God came to me again. He took me by the hand and said, "Today I am bringing you to the inner sanctuary, to the heart of God himself," and I was led to the Land of Laughter.'

14

The Four Friends

*... four men arrived, carrying a paralysed man to Jesus ...
seeing how much faith they had, Jesus said to the paralysed man,
'My son, your sins are forgiven.'*

Mk 2:3, 5.

'We'll never be the same again,' mused Moshe the village
tailor as he stood looking out at the moonlight on the lake.
The four were in Benyossef's house on the lake front talking
about the day's events in Capernaum.

'That will be him now,' said Abram, his eyes following a
small boat crossing the waters towards Tiberias. Abram, a
fisherman himself, had many the time seen the Master headed
in this direction before. 'He's away to the hills. What does he
do up there by himself?'

'Praying, I'm told,' said Benjamin the local carpenter and
jack-of-all-trades in the village, 'talking to the Father. He'll
have a lot to be saying to him tonight, I'm thinking.'

Reuben the local schoolmaster seemed as if he was still in
a trance. 'We have seen and heard wonderful things this
day,' he said gazing out into the night.

It all began in Moshe's shop. It was approaching midday
and word was about that the Master was in town. People
were already heading for Simon's house where he had spent
the night when Abram rushed in. 'Supposing we bring
Jonathan to him,' he exclaimed breathlessly, 'he might give
him back the use of his limbs. You round up Benjamin and

Reuben while I get him ready.' Jonathan their friend was paralysed from the waist down, the result of an accident. When the four arrived at the house carrying their friend on a pallet they soon realised that they hadn't a hope of getting in. The crowds were six deep around the door as they heaved and jostled to catch even a glimpse of the Master. There was a hush when the visitors from Judaea arrived wearing their long robes and broad phylacteries. As the crowd deferentially made way for them it became clear to Jonathan and his friends that these were the scribes and the pharisees. . . strange companions but intent on a common purpose, to meet the Master. The same respect was shown inside. The Master interrupted his discourse as people stood up offering their seats to the dignitaries from Jerusalem.

Meanwhile the four had taken Jonathan around to the back of the house where there were stone steps on to the roof. That night as they recalled what happened Benyossef took up the story. 'You know, I was in the house at the time. As the Master spoke we heard a disturbance on the roof. Next thing a hole appeared and pieces of dried earth and stones fell down through the rushes. Hassidah, Simon's mother-in-law rushed for a sweeping brush. Simon's language would have shocked the scribes but they were too busy brushing their long robes. Next thing the four of you were lowering Jonathan to the feet of Jesus.'

'We had a great view up there,' said Reuben, 'but did you notice that all eyes turned to the Master as if to say: will he cure Jonathan or not, whereas the Master was looking up at us smiling as if to say: well done lads, I admire your faith.'

'Yes,' said Benyossef, 'it was amusing to see the four of you peering down through the roof. Tell me, what impressed you most?'

'Well,' said Benjamin the first to speak, 'to be perfectly honest my first re-action was how I was going to face Simon and especially the mother-in-law over the damage done to the roof. But my fears went when the Master smiled up at us and I said to myself: What a man! Any man who can draw crowds like he does, any man with his healing powers must be special. I shall never forget what he did for Jonathan because I never thought that I would see that man on his feet again. Wasn't it great to see Jonathan prancing about with the pallet when the master healed him? Then again look at what happened this afternoon in the plaza. He got that scoundrel Levi to leave the tax table and follow him. I say it again: what a man!'

'Perhaps more than a man,' said Abram, 'could it be that he is the Messiah? Benyossef tells us the he had the scribes in all sorts of knots before we made our appearance as he trotted out one messianic line after the other. If he's not the Messiah then he must surely be one of the prophets!'

It was the turn of Reuben, the schoolmaster. 'More than a man, more than a prophet. This Jesus must surely be God!' His companions were startled but Reuben went on. 'Did you notice that two miracles were worked in Simon's house today? Did you see the relief on Jonathan's face when Jesus said to him: your sins are forgiven. It seemed as if a load had been lifted from him. Did you get the message? If you didn't, the scribes certainly did. He could read their minds. They didn't have to say it, he knew what they were thinking. He was assuming a divine power, only God can forgive sin. That's what they were thinking. So to prove that he had the power to forgive sin he worked that second miracle. He cured Jonathan. Sure you'd have to be blind not to get the message. God is no longer up there remote and inaccessible. He is here... he is Emmanuel, God with us. God is over there tonight in the hills of Tiberias in the person of the Nazarene.'

A strange silence settled on the little group as Reuben walked to the window and stood there looking in the direction of Tiberias. 'You know,' he said turning to his friends, 'we are living in wonderful times. Great things happened in Capernaum today. Blessed are our eyes to have seen what we witnessed and blessed are our ears to have heard lips pronounce the words we've all been waiting for, "your sins are forgiven". Think of our ancestors. They sinned against God.

Some of them repented and sacrificed burnt offerings, but there was no voice from God to tell them that they were forgiven. God's silence was oppressive... that is until today. I have a feeling that this is not the last time that human ears will hear human lips utter those healing words: your sins are forgiven.'

'And you Moshe,' said Benyossef, 'you've been very quiet all along. Is something troubling you?'

'Yes,' said the tailor, 'I suppose I should be jumping for joy like Jonathan, especially because of the part we played in today's events, but I'm bothered. I have a feeling that he signed his death-warrant today. He is a threat to the establishment and never more so than now. Why do you think they sent up that delegation from Jerusalem? Strange bedfellows the scribes and pharisees, but united in a common purpose, to get him, and get him they will. That claim to have divine powers was the last straw. They didn't come all the way from Jerusalem just to listen to the word. Did you hear that they had another go at him this afternoon when they found him eating with sinners. He'd be well advised to keep away from Jerusalem.'

On this sombre note the conversation ended. One by one the friends bade their farewells, Benjamin light-hearted as ever muttering, 'Got to fix that roof in the morning or I'll have the old mother-in-law breathing down my back!'

15

Preaching to the Broken-Hearted

To be human is necessarily to suffer. A world without suffering would be an engineered and hygienic hell.

DAVID DE VAY

In one of the classic poems of our times 'Lament for the Death of a Bullfighter' Lorca pictures his stricken hero mounting the steps *con todo su sufrimiento a cuestas* – with all his suffering on his shoulders. It is a picture of Christ carrying his cross and indeed a picture of us bearing on our shoulders our own sufferings or those of the ones we love.

The mystery of human suffering confronts us daily. How often do we go into homes feeling terribly inadequate trying to bring some measure of comfort to people in their troubles. How often on such a mission have I asked myself: what in God's name do I say to them? What do I say to a young couple who wake to find their first-born dead in the cot beside them? What do I say to a husband and father whose wife is slowly dying of cancer? How do I cope with the situation of a man killed on his way home from work? I enter the house and can smell his dinner in the oven as I break the news to his wife and family. Do I trot out cliches...? It's probably for the best. He's better off now. Don't take it so hard. Who are we to question the will of God? ... So often we priests are seen as representatives of the cruel God who took away a loved one.

Once a young boy was killed in a train accident and I had to preach at his funeral Mass. Confronted with the grief in the front seats my words sounded so hollow 'This is not a time

to be sad... In fact you should rejoice. Jim is taken away from
this world of sin and pain. He was taken away lest something
worse should happen to him!' Did I really expect Jim's
parents who were hurt and angry with God to rejoice at this
moment? And still the old cliches rolled out. 'God never
sends a burden greater then we can bear. He knows that you
are strong and that you can bear it!' Would you blame them
for thinking that if they had not been strong the accident
might never have happened?

Time and again we've all been accosted by people in
homes, hospitals, on the street, in airports: 'You're a priest,
tell me why does God...?' A man told me he had become an
atheist because he couldn't believe in a God who allows little
children to suffer. If he had been a real atheist he would have
not been so moved. His anger was directed against a God
who stayed aloof and did nothing.

Harold S. Kushner is a Jewish rabbi whose book *When Bad
Things Happen to Good People* is a world bestseller. It is a
father's attempt to make sense out of his son's suffering and
death, his own pain and the pain of others who have to
endure undeserved misfortune. Starting from the premise
that God does not will or cause suffering Kushner believes
that there is such a thing as randomness in the world, that
nature has it's laws but unfortunately not its values. So
lightning strikes a tree which falls and kills a passing motor-
ist; through being late I miss a plane which later crashes
killing everyone on board.

Human nature alas rejects the notion of random suffering.
We are forever looking for causes. If we don't blame God, we
blame ourselves. Guilt like anger is a recurring reaction to the
problem of human suffering: What did I do wrong? What did
I do to deserve this? If only I hadn't let her go for that
operation. If... If... If.

The God I believe in does not send us the problem. He
gives us the strength to cope with the problem and he usually
does this through people, people who care and who are his
lips and his hands and feet in bringing comfort and hope

when we feel like cracking under the pain. Six year old Sally got it right. One day she came in late for lunch and explained to her mum that she'd been comforting Mrs Kennedy who had lost her husband. When her mother asked what she did to bring comfort to the bereaved widow, Sally replied, 'I just sat on her lap and cried with her.'

Some priests attract people from far and near by their sheer holiness. Father John is one of these. He is pastor of a remote country parish where people keep coming to him for comfort and advice and to have him 'Pray over' them. They also come for healing, physical as well as spiritual, and some were not slow in attributing miraculous powers to him. The most daunting challenge he ever faced came from a very distraught woman. She had lost her only son and she came to Father John seeking a miracle. 'You have the ear of God,' she cried, 'He'll listen to you. Ask him to give me back my son. I can't live without him.'

Now John didn't do what I might have done. He didn't sit her down and theologise with her. Instead he told her to go first and come back to him with a piece of bread from a house which had not experienced suffering. 'When you do,' he said, 'I promise you that I shall put your case to the Lord.'

The woman went away and her first call was to a stately home which bore all the trappings of wealth and happiness. To her surprise she found the family going through the pangs of bereavement. She stayed some time with them sharing her own feelings of loss and unconsciously bringing comfort and strength to the stricken household. She moved on to a poor man's cottage to find the peasant and his wife mourning the death of their five year old girl killed as she ran out on the road after her dog. Here again she identified with the suffering of the bereaved couple and again there was mutual consolation and comfort. In another house she found a woman whose character was ruined by malicious gossip. In home after home the story was the same, there was no house without its share of suffering. She found that in the process of visiting and talking about her pain and the pain of others she was healed. People, ordinary human beings who have experienced life's hurts can so often be God's language to a sick and suffering society.

Recently the people of our community went to the Marian shrine of Knock to spend a night in prayer for healing for a young mother dying of cancer. Right through the night they opened their hearts in prayer to avert a tragedy. The prayers went apparently unanswered. There was no miracle. Sadie died on schedule leaving a family bereft of wife and mother. Were our prayers really unanswered? I think not. I spoke to Sadie shortly before she died and she told me that she felt the strength of a faith community around her and of a God beside her helping her to cope with a situation that might easily have broken her spirit. In this sense her prayers and ours were answered.

The God I believe in did not create human suffering nor does he will it. The evil in the world, the horrors perpetrated by the Hitlers, Stalins and Idi Amins of our own times were not caused by God but by human beings with free-will who chose to be cruel to their fellow men. Why didn't God intervene? If he did he would take away the very freedom that makes us human.

Does God know what it means to suffer? Does he know or care about those who are complaining against him? If we really understand the Incarnation, that God became human, that he freely chose a life of suffering then we might make some sense out of the problem of evil in our world. Does the God of Bethlehem know anything about being homeless? Does the God of Bethany know anything about malicious tongues? Does the God of the Lithostrotos know anything about rejection and betrayal? Does the God of Gethsemane know anything about loneliness? Does the God of Calvary know anything of death and dying and the open wounds of accident wards, of cancer and the like? Of course he does. He's been through it all. He has taught us that to be human is to suffer and that there might be a divine purpose in all of it.

The following scenario tell it all:

At the end of time, billions of people were scattered on a great plain before God's throne. Most shrank back from the brilliant light before them. But some groups near the front talked heatedly – not with cringing shame, but with belligerence.

'Can God judge us? How can he know about suffering?' snapped a pert young brunette. She ripped open a sleeve to reveal a tattooed number from a Nazi concentration camp. 'We endured terror, beatings, torture, death!'

In another group a Negro boy lowered his collar. 'What about this?' he demanded, showing an ugly rope burn. 'Lynched...for no crime but being black!'

In another crowd, a pregnant schoolgirl with sullen eyes. 'Why should I suffer,' she murmured, 'it wasn't my fault.'

Far out across the plain there were hundreds of such groups. Each had a complaint against God for the evil and suffering he permitted in his world. How lucky God was to live in heaven where all was sweetness and light, where there was no weeping or fear, no hunger or hatred. What did God know of all that man had been forced to endure in this world? For God leads a pretty sheltered life, they said.

So each of these groups sent forth their leader, chosen because he had suffered the most. A Jew, a Negro, a person from Hiroshima, a horribly deformed arthritic, a thalidomide child. In the centre of the plain they consulted with each other. At last they were ready to present their case. It was rather clever.

Before God could be qualified to be their judge, he must endure what they had endured. The decision was that God should be sentenced to live on earth – as a man!

'Let him be born a Jew. Let the legitimacy of his birth be doubted. Give him work so difficult that even his family will think him out of his mind when he tries to do it. Let him be betrayed by his closest friends. Let him face false charges, be tried by a prejudiced jury and convicted by a cowardly judge. Let him be tortured.

'At the last, let him see what it means to be terribly alone. Then let him die. Let him die so that there can be no doubt that he died. Let there be a great host of witnesses to verify it.'

As each leader announced his portion of the sentence, loud murmurs of approval went up from the throng of people assembled.

And when the last had finished pronouncing sentence, there was a long silence. No one uttered another word. No one moved. For suddenly all knew that God had already served his sentence.

THE PEOPLE GOD FORGOT – This was the graphic front-page headline of a British newspaper reporting on the Armenian earthquake disaster. Here was a deeply religious people who must have wondered if God had forsaken them. For weeks before the calamity thousands of those who died had fled their homes to escape persecution by the Moslem Azerbaijanis; seventy years ago one and a half million Armenians were slaughtered in a bloody act of genocide by the Moslem Turks. As one victim of the earthquake wandered traumatised through that wasteland which obliterated homes and families and friends he was heard to murmur 'Now it seems that even God is against us!' It was a *cri du coeur* to a God who stood aloof from the inexorable laws of nature and the apocalyptic forces that surge and boil beneath the crust of the earth. Suddenly political issues such as military balance and international protocol seemed irrelevant. Within hours differences were forgotten and the whole world was in touch, all drawn together to cope with natural catastrophe. It was one of those moments of poignant paradox where hope could be seen through tears.

16

The Shadow of the Cross

I will boast only about the cross of our Lord Jesus Christ.
                                    GALATIANS 6:14

There is a famous painting by Holman Hunt entitled *The Shadow of Death*. It depicts the inside of Joseph's carpenter's shop at Nazareth. Stripped to the waist Jesus stands by a wooden bench on which he has put down his saw. It is the end of the day and he is tired. He stretches his arms and as he does so the evening sunlight coming through the open door casts a dark shadow in the form of a cross on the wall behind him. His tool-rack on the wall now looks like a horizontal bar on which his hands have been pierced. The tools become grim reminders of the hammer and nails of Calvary.

In the left foreground of the picture Mary kneels amid the wood chippings looking sadly at the cross-like shadow on the wall. Ever since that fateful day in the Temple when Simeon prophesied 'Thine own soul a sword shall piece' the cross cast it's shadow ahead of her son. His death was central to his mission and he was forever reminding his followers of his impending death. We read in the first gospel: 'Then Jesus began to teach his disciples: "The Son of Man must suffer much and be rejected by the elders, the chief priests and the teachers of the law. He will be put to death, but three days later he will rise to life" (Mk 8:31).'

The first creed of the early chruch gave top priority to the cross. The very first article of faith as enunciated by St Paul is 'I passed on to you what I received, which is of the greatest importance: that Christ died for our sins, as written in the Scriptures' (1 Cor 15:3). It was at the very core of the apostles' preaching. 'For while I was with you, I made up my mind to forget everything except Jesus Christ and especially his death on the cross' (1 Cor 2:2) – Paul writing to the Corinthians.

When we consider that the cross is the universal symbol of our Christian faith, its centrality in the life of Christ and the teaching and preaching of the early Church, and how it dominates the entire New Testament we must seriously question the part it plays in our homilies and preaching. More often than not it is confined to the Good Friday slot. The reading of the Passion on Palm Sunday is often an excuse for not preaching a homily and indeed the manner in which it is read can often add to the sense of foreboding with which many congregations face this annual endurance test.

It must be said however that, in many of our churches, audience participation in the Passion narrative and in the Stations of the Cross has given a new dimension to the events of Good Friday. The people have been challenged to ask themselves how they would have stood in relation to the trial and the crucifixion of Jesus. With which character in the narrative would I identify myself? Was I there when they crucified my Lord?

'We readers or hearers are meant to participate,' writes Raymond Brown, 'by asking ourselves how we would have stood in relation to the trial and crucifixion of Jesus. With which character in the narrative would I identify myself? The distribution of palm in church may too quickly assure me that I would have been among the crowd that hailed Jesus appreciatively. Is it not more likely that I might have been among the disciples who fled from danger, abandoning him? Or at moments in my life have I not played the role of Peter, denying Jesus, or even Judas betraying him. Have I not found myself like Johannine Pilate, trying to avoid a decision between good and evil? Or like the Matthean Pilate have I made a bad decision and then washed my hands so that the record could show that I was blameless? Or most likely of all, might I not have stood among the religious leaders who condemned Jesus?'

But apart from the Holy Week liturgies the Scripture readings on the other Sundays provide ample opportunities for speaking about the Cross. People have a right to be told what it means and its transforming power to give a new relationship to God, a new understanding of ourselves, a new incentive to give ourselves in mission, a new love for our enemies, a new grasp of the meaning of the Mass and a new courage to face the perplexities of suffering.

Let us cast one final glance at the scene on the afternoon of Good Friday. It may tell us something because all of us in the course of our lives experience some sort of Calvary. Jesus did not die alone. There were three crosses on the hill that Friday afternoon.

There was the cross of rejection. On it hung the unrepentant thief. If ever there was an instance of wasted pain this was it. The blood of redemption was trickling to the ground beside him, in one cry for mercy he could have been saved but instead he chose to vent his anger on God. Anger is an understandable reaction to the Cross provided it does not close the door to acceptance. It may even open the door as for instance in these stories. Christy Nolan born a spastic signed to his father to wheel him into a Dublin church and there summoning what feeble strength he had lifted his crippled arms and made an obscene gesture to the crucified Christ. Then laughing at the absurdity of it all, he found inner peace and acceptance.

A fine illustration of the same kind of release is to be found in a powerful novel by Peter de Vries, *The Blood of the Lamb*. A man goes into a church on his way to the hospital to see his daughter who is dying of leukaemia; he has gone to pray for her recovery; it is the child's birthday and he takes with him a birthday cake. He arrives at the hospital to find the child dying. In less than an hour she is dead. He returns to the church and throws the cake at the crucifix and in that action finds his release.

So often the cross we carry is one of rejection. We carry bitterness in our hearts down all our days and unlike Christy Nolan we fail to see the absurdity of it all.

Then there was the Cross of acceptance. The good thief was rather special. He was the last person to speak a kind word to Christ. The Cross for him had the purifying effect of leading him to an acknowledgement of his sinfulness and his need of God's saving mercy. He made one cry for mercy and in that cry he was saved.

In the centre was the Cross of redemption on which hung the one 'by whose wounds we were healed'. This is the unique Cross yet Paul spoke to the Colossians of 'filling up' what was lacking of the afflictions of Christ. By some strange paradox the Lord can take our crosses and turn them to redemptive use.

The Abbey of the Holy Cross is one of the jewels in the crown of Ireland. Shortly after it became a Cistercian foundation in the twelfth century a young Plantagenet prince, the son of Henry I of England and Queen Eleanor of Aquitaine, came to Ireland to take up the Pope's Peter's Pence collection. Despite their respect for the Holy Father, the collection and the Plantagenets were anathema to a fierce Tipperary clan called the O'Fogartys who murdered the prince as soon as he set foot in the county. They buried the body in a secret place but the story goes that one of the monks in the Abbey had a dream in which he saw a hand sticking up out of the earth. He hurried from his cell to inform the Abbot who roused a few other monks to accompany him in the search for the body. When they found it they carried it back and reverently buried it in the Abbey chapel. To this day it is known as the Tomb of the Good Woman's Son. Eleanor, the Good Woman rewarded the monks by giving them a sizeable portion of the True Cross discovered by St Helena. For centuries pilgrims came to the Abbey in their thousands to be blessed with the relic. Badly damaged during the Protestant Reformation, the Abbey is now restored to its former splendour; the relic is back in the sanctuary facing the Tomb of the Good Woman's Son and the pilgrims are also back in their thousands. The most striking feature of the restored chapel is the altar hewn from solid rock and cut into it in golden capitals the words *Ut Non Evacuetur Crux Christi* – lest the Cross of Christ be deprived of its power.

There is our awesome task as preachers of the word – to ensure that the Cross will never be deprived of its power.

Some would argue that the heart of the meaning of the Cross is that Christ took our place. Here is a telling illustration. A boy was consistently late coming home from school and could give no convincing explanation or excuse to his parents for his tardiness. Driven to desperation his father sat him down one evening and solemnly admonished him that if ever he was late again he would be put on a bread and water diet. The warning was to no avail and the following evening the boy arrived home even later than usual, needless to say to a chilly reception. His mother refused to speak to him as also did his dad. Came meal time and to his dismay he saw that his parents carried out their threat. The other plates were piled high with food but all that was set before him was a glass of water and one slice of dry bread. His father waited until the full impact had sunk in, then he switched places taking the bread and water himself and placing his own dinner in front of the boy. The youth never forgot what his father had done in taking upon himself the punishment that was his by right. Years later he recalled the incident and said, 'All my life I've known what God is like by what my father did that night.'

Another true story with a similar message tells of a Russian General, the Governor of a province in one of the Soviet Republics. Concerned with the outbreak of a rash of petty crimes he issued an edict that anyone caught and convicted would receive one hundred lashes. As fate would have it the first person to be arrested under the new edict was the

General's own mother. She had been caught pilfering in a shop. He was in a terrible dilemma torn by the need to uphold the law and his love for his mother. The villagers assembled in the market-place for the flogging and just as his mother's hands were being tied to the post the General stepped forward, released her, pushed her gently aside, bared his back and took the one hundred lashes in her stead.

17

In the Power of the Spirit

The Gospel is preached in the ears of all; it only comes with power to some. The power that is in the Gospel does not lie in the eloquence of the preacher; otherwise men would be converters of souls. Nor does it lie in the preacher's learning; otherwise it would consist in the wisdom of men. . . We might as well preach to stone walls as preach to humanity unless the Holy Spirit be with the word, to give it power to convert the soul.

C. H. SPURGEON

Spurgeon belongs to a vanished breed. He was one of the great princes of the pulpit. The dominant feature of the Church in London where he preached to chock-a-block congregations was a massive central pulpit with fifteen steps leading up to it in a great sweeping curve. It is said that Spurgeon as he mounted those stairs used to pause on each step and say, 'I believe in the Holy Spirit'. By the time he entered the pulpit he did believe in the Spirit and he spoke in his power.

Shortly before he died Pope John was asked what Church doctrine needed most re-emphasis today. He replied, 'The doctrine of the Holy Spirit.' The Holy Spirit gets a slot in our preaching at Pentecost and Confirmation time. He deserves better especially since our entire preaching is inexplicable and impossible without him.

We need him if only as Simon Tugwell points out 'to free us from our dumbness'. We need to tell our people who he is, what he does, where he came from and what he is doing in the world today.

When Paul introduced the Christian faith to Europe one of his first ports of call was Thessalonika, the modern city of Salonika. He begins the first of his letters to the Christian community of Thessalonika with the words, 'Our gospel came to you not simply with words, but also with power, with the Holy Spirit and with deep conviction.' Unless our preaching comes with power and the Holy Spirit and deep conviction we are wasting our time. This calls for continual dependence on the presence and power of the Spirit in every phase of homily preparation and delivery. If the preparation consists of reaching for pre-packaged homily hints while watching television on Friday or Saturday evenings, then don't count on the Holy Spirit being part of that operation.

The same holds for the delivery of the homily. Have you ever had the feeling that despite hours of careful preparation your words suddenly fall flat? This can happen particularly in situations where one has to preach at more than one Mass on Sundays. You can sense the gilt wearing off in the repeat performance. To assume that no preparation is necessary the second time around is a recipe for disaster. We need the Holy Spirit each time to be able to say to ourselves at the end of the homily: This is the word of the Lord.

Today people are talking more about the Holy Spirit and more books have been written about him, thanks mainly to the influence of the charismatic movement. Preachers must resist the temptation that because they are so open to the Spirit in the renewal movement they need little or no preparation in constructing their homilies. All of us without exception need the Spirit to illuminate our minds to the truth in conscientious preparation and to empower us before and during the delivery of the message. There is no evidence that the Holy Spirit favours spur-of-the-moment oratory to prayerful and painstaking preparation.

The story is told of a student for the ministry who assured his professor of homiletics that he was guided by the Holy Spirit in his preaching. After one rather inept performance he received the caustic advice, 'Next time you're in touch with the Spirit how about asking him to guide you to the library.'

Another preacher who did not prepare his sermons because of his confidence in the Holy Spirit appealed to Scripture to support his case. 'Have you not read Matthew 10:19-20?' he chided one of his colleagues, 'Do not worry about what you are going to say or how you will say it; when the time comes you will be given what you will say. For the words you will speak will not be yours; they will come from the Spirit of your Father speaking through you.' He was somewhat taken aback when it was pointed out to him that the words quoted were out of context. The preceding verse was 'you will be brought to trial before rulers and kings and ...when they bring you to trial, do not worry about what you are going to say...' The words he quoted referred to the law courts not the Sunday homily!

I cannot recall where I read that if the Holy Spirit were taken out of Catholic practice today ninety-five percent of what we are doing would continue and no one would know the difference. We'd still keep all the external observances, Mass, Sacraments, Novenas, Pilgrimages, etc.

If on the other hand the Holy Spirit had to be taken from the religious practice of the early Church ninety-five percent of what they were at would cease immediately and everyone would feel the difference. Just recall some of his dramatic interventions after Pentecost. Not long after that great beginning, Peter, John and their friends were praying when the house in which they were gathered was rocked as they were filled with the Holy Spirit for the *second time* (Acts 4:31). The Spirit came upon Cornelius, his relatives and friends as they listened to the message from Peter (Acts 10:44-48). Then there was the case of those at Ephesus who had known only the baptism of John. Luke tells us that they received a fresh baptism and the laying on of hands followed by the gift of the Spirit (Acts 19: 5-6).

There's a story about the martyr St Lucy. When she was on trial for her life the Roman judge asked her what it was that gave her the courage to defy the might of the Roman Empire and face martyrdom for her Christian beliefs. Lucy's reply baffled him. 'I am not afraid to die because the Spirit of God lives in me and my body is in very truth the shrine of God.' Leonidas, father of the great Christian writer Origen whilst still a catechumen used to kneel by the bedside of his sleeping son and reverently kiss his breast as the temple in which the Spirit dwelt.

Somewhere along the line in the Church's struggle for recognition, privilege and ultimately control an attempt was made to legislate for the Holy Spirit. He was conveniently slotted into Confirmation but as John V. Taylor points out in *The Go-Between God*, 'The Holy Spirit does not appear to have read the rubrics. He will not and cannot be bound.' He goes on, 'Of course the Church must lay down its norms for doctrine and practice but we should be as ready as the weather forecaster to admit that however reliable our calculations most of the time, we cannot command the wind. And when the Spirit disobeys our canons we should avoid the absurd sin of rigidity!' Priests and preachers in the charismatice renewal movement would surely say 'Amen' to this!

One of the paradoxes of our faith is that it is in the real absence that we often experience the real presence. So unpredicatable is the Spirit that the moment of vision and rebirth can come when we are in the pits of depression and despair. The breaking down of our defences is a pre-requisite for a renewal of the Holy Spirit.

The moment of highest drama in Tolstoy's *The Power of Darkness* comes when the villain Nikita who just wedded his master's wife suddenly leaves the festivities and goes out into the night with the intention of doing away with himself. His new bride had poisoned her sickly husband and Nikita in turn had seduced her sixteen year old step-daughter and murdered the baby at birth. He staggers in despair through the darkness and in the yard stumbles over the drunken form of Mitrich the old soldier and jack-of-all-trades. Tolstoy paints a vivid picture of the two kneeling in the stinking straw weeping on each others shoulders.

For Nikita it is the unlikely moment of vision and renewal.
It comes when the old soldier cries, 'I love you, but you are
a fool. You think I'm a warrior? No, I'm not a warrior, I'm the
very least of men, a poor lost orphan. Well then do you think
I'm afraid of you? No fear! I'm afraid of no man. As I don't
fear men. I'm easy!' For any onlooker it would appear like a
drunken scene as Pentecost did to the onlookers but for the
guilty Nikita it was a moment of conversion and re-birth.
'You tell me not to fear men?' he asks, springing to his feet.

'Why fear such muck as they are?' answers Mitrich, 'You
look at 'em in the bath-house. All made of one paste!'

Nikita rushes back to the wedding party and as he makes
his confession to the guests his old father cries out in ecstasy,
'God! God! It is here!'

Taylor uses Tolstoy's story to illustrate the Spirit 'blowing
where he wills', and concludes in masterly fashion: 'It is
worth remembering that the root of the words humiliation
and humility is *humus*. To be down in the straw and the dung
and the refuse – Paul's words – is to become the soil in which
the seed of Christ's manhood falls and dies and brings forth
the harvest. Here is the meeting of the four elements: we, the
earth and the Spirit, the wind the water and the fire.'

The first step towards renewal is to acknowledge the
presence of sin in my life, to recognise the obstacles and
barriers that block the work of the Holy Spirit and to do
something about them.

A young priest assigned to his first parish was in the habit
of taking a walk in the countryside every afternoon. His
itinerary took him past neat tidy farmsteads, well tilled fields
and green pastures where cattled grazed. The entire scene
was idyllic except for one small holding. It was a wasteland,
desolate and abandoned, with weeds and brambles making
access to the unoccupied house difficult. The paddock in
front of the dwelling was covered with noxious weeds,
nettles and rocks and was being used as a dumping ground
for garbage. It was an eye-sore and the priest couldn't stand

the sight of it. In due course he moved to another parish and twenty years later he was back again in his first parish, this time as parish priest.

On his first stroll through the countryside he came on a sight wondrous to behold. The ugly scene had vanished. The old house was painted and re-roofed. The weeds, rocks and brambles had disappeared and were replaced by nicely laid out lawns with shrubs and flower-beds. The rocks that had littered the place previously were now part of a rock-garden at the entrance of which was a linden tree, a symbol of re-birth. As he gazed in wonder and admiration the priest noticed the new owner watering the flowers. He introduced himself and said: 'I cannot tell you how happy I am to see what you and the Lord have done to this place.'

'Thank you, father,' the man replied, 'but I wish you could have seen it when the Lord had it all to himself.'

Cardinal Mercier had these words of wisdom for his priests. 'I am going to reveal to you a secret of sanctity and happiness. If every day during five minutes you will keep your imagination quiet, shut your eyes to all the things of sense, and close your ears to all the sounds of earth so as to be able to withdraw into the sanctuary of your baptised soul which is the Temple of the Holy Spirit saying:

O Holy Spirit, soul of my soul, I adore you;
Enlighten, guide, strengthen and console me.
Tell me what I ought to do and command me to do it.
I promise to be submissive in everything that you shall ask me
And to accept all that you permit to happen to me.
Only show me you will.

'If you do this your life will pass happily and serenely; con-solation will abound even in the midst of troubles for grace will be given in proportion to the trial as well as strength to bear it bringing you to the gates of Paradise full of merit. This submission to the Holy Spirit is the secret of sanctity.'

The necessary submission of preacher and preaching to

the Holy Spirit is the final evidence that our preaching can enlighten the minds and put fire into the hearts of our listeners.

18

Looking Heavenwards

*I hope there are going to be football games and a cup tie in Heaven.
Sorry if that sounds flippant, but I don't want it just to be all angels
and wings. It's going to be full of life for me. Me with others, and all
of us in some wonderful way together.*

NEVILLE BLACK

One of the great movies on the Second World War tells the
story of the five Sullivan brothers. All of them were assigned
to the same battleship and all of them lost their lives in a naval
battle in the Pacific. The film ends with the brothers walking
hand in hand on fleecy clouds towards the pearly gates to the
accompaniment of celestial music and a Hollywood heavenly choir. That is how I saw Heaven as a child, clouds and
harps and wings, a place where people spent their time being
good and singing holy songs. Heaven as thus imagined
wasn't particularly desirable but it was so much better than
going to Hell. As a matter of fact I wasn't headed anywhere.
My steady gaze was fixed on the fires of Hell and what I was
really doing was backing into eternal happiness.

The seminary did little to clarify or enhance my concept of
Heaven. I was taught that the essential happiness of Heaven
consisted in the Beatific Vision. Happiness in the dismal
decade of the 1940s was tied up with material things, the end
of rationing, to have a car and plenty of money, to buy the
good things of life. The mind was incapable of grasping
eternal realities. Then I delved into the Scriptures to see what
God had in store for me and three things emerged to clarify
my vision of the future life.

First, Heaven is a home – 'for us our homeland is in Heaven'. This meant a lot to me. Home is a place of love and comfort and warmth. In Revelation it is described as a City. That meant people, lots of them. So it was not unreasonable to expect that at least part of our happiness would consist in that which meant so much to us on earth – companionship. It meant being re-united with those near and dear to me. The Negro spiritual 'Going Home' said it all, God wants me to want Heaven, not just to regard it as the grim alternative to the everlasting bonfire.

Secondly, Heaven consists in the absence of all evil. The vision of John on Patmos brought great comfort: 'He will wipe away all tears from their eyes. There will be no more death, no more grief or crying or pain. The old things have disappeared' (Rev 21:4). What a wonderful prospect – no more suffering, no more partings, no more death, no more insecurity. Our greatest happiness on earth is so often haunted by insecurity, the fear of losing a loved one, the fear of cancer, the fear of unemployment, the collapse of ones fortunes. These inbuilt imperfections would have no place in a state of perfect happiness.

All this led to the third point that the essential happiness of Heaven consists in the possession of all good, that only in God would the hopes, aspirations and dreams of the human heart be realised. The words of Augustine became crystal clear: Thou hast made us for thyself, O Lord and our hearts shall never rest until they rest in thee.

'To see God face to face. . ,' says Hunter, 'amid the fellowship of the Church triumphant, this surely is the end of all ends, the final solution to life's riddle and the consummation of all love and desire.'

In the *Confessions*, Augustine describes a memorable evening in Ostia with his mother Monica. As they talked of things spiritual they felt that they had left time behind. 'Still higher did we climb by the staircase of the Spirit, thinking and speaking of you and marvelling at your works, O Lord. And as we talked and yearned, we touched the life for an instant with the full force of our hearts.' In this instant, mother and son had a foretaste of life in Heaven and an insight into what John meant when he said 'This is eternal life.'

One final reminder. The best of illustrations have their limitations. None of them is complete. At best they serve to illustrate, to shed some light. This is especially true of illustrations and stories about Heaven. With fantasy pouring in continuously and variously from every direction it is difficult to accept and to hold on to God as our last end. What follows may serve to illustrate, to shed some light on something that is beyond our human comprehension but is nevertheless the goal towards which we are all striving.

Innisfree is a lake island in Ireland, so beautiful that it inspired W. B. Yeats' most famous poem. Once upon a time a holy man lived out all his days on this island which for him was a reflection of Heaven itself. When the time came for him to die he had his friends bring him outside and lay him on his beloved earth. Just as he was about to expire he reached down and clasped a handful of earth.

When he presented himself at Heaven's gate Peter greeted him, 'Come in friend, we've all been waiting for you. . . but first you must let go that handful of soil.'

'Never,' said the holy man, and Peter sadly left him outside the gate.

A few eons went by. Peter came out again, this time bringing with him Ireland's national apostle St Patrick. The holy man was overjoyed to meet the great saint, they sat and talked about the old country and as Patrick got up to leave he said, 'Come back in with me, We have some wonderful surprises in store for you but first get rid of that soil that you are holding.' The holy man again refused and stayed outside.

More eons rolled by, Peter came out once more. This time the Lord himself was with him. The Lord looked kindly at him and said, 'Come on in son, we all miss you. We have prepared something special for you.' By this time the holy man was old and feeble. The Lord and Peter helped him to his feet, he leaned heavily upon them and as they approached the gate his strength gave out, the fingers of his fist gradually loosened and the soil began to filter out between them until his hand was empty.

He then entered Heaven and there before his eyes was his beloved Innisfree!

The Lord was never lonely when Danny was around. He was first into the church in the morning and was an altar boy for four score years and when he retired after a lifetime of teaching the extra time was given exclusively to God. Like many another committed Christian Danny had gone through the crucible of suffering. He had watched his wife and seven of his children die and death was now beckoning to himself. Shortly before the final summons I sat by his bedside and we talked about Heaven. I told him how much I envied him the welcome that awaited him and was more than a little taken aback by his response. 'I'm not so sure,' he said as he leafed through a thumbworn prayer book. Memoriam cards of his loved ones fell out of the book and on to the bed-clothes before he found what he was looking for, a small sheet of paper with a few hand written verses. 'Read that,' he said handing me the sheet, 'it says it all.' I copied the verses. They went like this:

> I dreamt I died the other night
> and Heaven's gates swung open wide
> An angel with a halo bright
> ushered me inside.
> And there to my astonishment
> Stood folk that I had labelled,
> As quite unfit, of little worth
> And spiritually disabled.
> Indignant words rose to my lips
> But never were set free,
> For every face showed stunned surprise
> Not one expected me!

Danny's elegy recalled Vachel Londray's sensational poem 'General William Booth Enters Heaven'. It is graphic description of the tumultuous welcome which General William Booth received in Heaven from the criminals, fornicators, drunkards and prostitutes who had been saved through The Salvation Army. It caused an uproar at the time and was condemned by the respectable colony of the blameless who were outraged to think that Heaven was inhabited by saved sots and convicted harlots. Some of us are in for the surprise of our lives!

One evening a little girl was walking with her Father on an evening stroll. The little girl was looking up at the stars as she clasped her father's hand. 'Daddy,' she said, 'if the bottom side of Heaven is so beautiful what must it be like inside!' The father caught a glimpse of Heaven in the enraptured face of his child who at that moment was walking knee-deep in stardust and helping her dad take hold of the hand of God.

Once there was a holy hermit who took himself away from the world and lived a life of strict asceticism on a daily diet of bread and water. He imposed the same penitential exercises on a young disciple who had accompanied him. Despite the rigorous austerities which he practiced he was tormented with sexual thoughts and desires. Night after night when he had dreams of naked women running about his cell he would rouse himself from sleep, take the lash and chastise his body into subjection. He was not amused when the disciple suggested respectfully to him that if he suspended his diet and partook of an occasional beef-steak that the temptresses might disappear. The holy man continued with his austerities until the Lord called him home and the disciple unable to cope with his loneliness soon followed him. Shortly after entering the next life the disciple came upon his master with a beautiful young lady sitting on his lap. 'Ah Father,' he exclaimed, 'the Lord has brought you to Heaven and rewarded you for your struggle against temptation.'

'Shut up, you fool,' said the holy man, 'this is not Heaven...
and besides, she's the one who is being punished.'

Fulton Sheen told a good story about an occasion when he
went to deliver a lecture in a certain town. Having parked his
car he came on a group of small boys kicking a ball about the
car-park. When he asked them for directions to the town hall
one precocious kid queried, 'Watcha want to go to the town
hall for?'

'I'm going to tell some people how to get to Heaven,'
replied the bishop, adding, 'Now son how would you like to
come along and let me show you the way to Heaven?'

'G'wan,' said the kid as he returned to the ball-game, 'you
don't even know the way to the townhall!'

There's a story of a little girl who was told that if she was
good she would go to Heaven when she died and live with
the angels. The child showed a refreshingly candid grasp of
eternal bliss by asking whether, if she was very good, they
would let her have a little devil to play with.

Once a village blacksmith had a vision. An angel came to
tell him that God was calling him home to the fullness of the
Kingdom.

'I thank God for thinking of me,' replied the blacksmith,
'but as you know, the season for sowing the crops is beginning and, as I am the only blacksmith in these parts, who will
help these poor people when a horse needs to be shod, or a
plough needs to be fixed? I don't wish to appear ungrateful,
but do you think I could put off taking my place in the
Kingdom until I have finished?'

'I'll see what can be done,' said the angel, as he vanished.
The angel returned a year or two later with the same message. This time, however, a farmer was seriously ill, and the
blacksmith was trying to save his crop for him, so that his
family wouldn't suffer. The angel was sent back to see what
could be done.

This happened again and again, and on each occasion the blacksmith just spread his hands in a gesture of resignation and compassion, and drew the angel's attention to where the suffering was, and where his help was needed. Eventually, the blacksmith felt very old and tired, and he prayed, 'Lord, if you would like to send your angel again, I think I'd be happy to see him.'

The angel appeared. 'If you still want to take me,' said the blacksmith, 'I am ready to take up my abode in the Lord's Kingdom.'

The angel looked at the blacksmith in surprise and said, 'where do you think you've been all those years?'

Peter frowned as he watched the Rake approach the pearly gates. 'Be off you malingerer,' he said, 'there is no place for you here.'

'But Peter, he may look kindly on me. Remember how he looked at you that night in the courtyard when you swore by high heaven that you did not know him.'

Peter blanched and the Rake pressing home his advantage went on, 'I may have robbed, and plundered, Peter, but I never denied the faith!'

'All right, all right,' said Peter, wishing to put an end to the exchange, 'You can enter, but you'd better get some high-ranking person to plead your case in the Judgment Hall. I'd suggest one of the four evangelists seeing that your fate may well depend on their written words.'

He accompanied the Rake to the abode of the evangelists. The countenance of the four did nothing to reassure the Rake as they perused his file. Then Matthew spoke: 'I'm afraid your record is too bad. . .'

Before he could deliver a verdict the Rake came back at him. 'Remember Matthew when you were called Levi. Didn't you too rob and cheat when you sold out to the Roman oppressors. And yet, even as you collected the hated taxes that day in Capernaum did he not call you into his kingdom? Surely there must be a place in that kingdom for me!'

Then he turned to Mark. 'Who are you Mark to accuse me of being a trouble-maker? You too were a mischief-maker. Remember how difficult you made life for Paul! Remember the rift you caused between him and Barnabas! And yet you were the first to write about the Kingdom!

'As for you, John,' he continued, addressing the beloved disciple. 'You were in a privileged position on earth. You were with him on Tabor. But there was no end to your ambition. You wanted a position of privilege up here too. Remember when he was lonely and depressed that night in Gethsemane? You don't, because you slept right through it!'

Matthew smirked at John's discomfiture but the Rake was now addressing Luke. 'When I look at you, Luke, my heart is filled with hope. You wrote about a Christ who was the friend of sinners; yours was the Gospel of the underdog. Only in your book did I read about the kind Samaritan, the sinner in the Temple who went out justified, the lost son and the waiting father. I am the lost son. . . the lost sheep. . . but I feel that there is a place for me in the kingdom. Can you see it in your heart to plead my case?'

And Luke smile as he approached the Rake. 'Of course I can,' he said putting his arm around the other's shoulders. 'Come with me, and let me assure you in advance that there will be joy in heaven when I tell them your story.'

By way of valedicatory let us reflect together on the thoughts of Dr Samuel Johnson as he looked heavenwards. The dominant aspect of his life only superficially covered by his friends and biographers was his religion, his undeviating commitment to Christ. Before he died Boswell his biographer expressed surprise that such an estimable and distinguished citizen should be overlooked when filling important posts in the realm and denied the praise that was his due. Johnson's response to such worldly values comes in the words of his alter ego, the Sage in his enchanting story *Rasselas:*

'Praise,' said the sage, with a sigh, 'is to an old man an

empty sound. I have neither mother to be delighted with the reputation of her son, nor wife to partake of the honours of her husband. I have outlived my friends and my rivals. Nothing is now of much importance; for I cannot extend my interest beyond myself. Youth is delighted with applause, because it is considered as the earnest of some future good, and because the prospect of life is far extended: but to me, who am now declining to decrepitude, there is little to be feared from the malevolence of men, and yet less to be hoped from their affection or esteem. Something they may yet take away, but they can give me nothing. Riches would now be useless, and high employment would be pain. My retrospect of life recalls to my view many opportunities of good neglected, much time squandered upon trifles, and more lost in idleness and vacancy. I leave many great designs unattempted, and many great attempts unfinished. My mind is burdened with no heavy crime, and therefore I compose myself to tranquillity; endeavour to abstract my thoughts from hopes and cares, which, though reason knows them to be vain, still try to keep their old possession of the heart; expect with serene humility that hour which nature cannot long delay; and hope to possess, in a better state, that happiness which here I could not find, and that virtue which here I have not attained.'

May these splendid sentiments of Johnson find an echo in your heart as they have in mine.

Bibliography

Walter M. Abbott SJ and Joseph Gallagher (editors), *The Documents of Vatican Two*, Geoffrey Chapman, London-Dublin 1966.

William J. Bausch, *Storytelling - Imagination and Faith*, Twenty-Third Publications, Mystic, Connectitcut, 1984.

Bible Societies, *Good News Bible*, Swindon, 1976.

Bishops' Committee on Priestly Life and Ministry -*Fulfilled in Your Hearing, The Homily in the Sunday Assembly*, United States Catholic Conference, 1984.

Raymond E. Brown, *A Crucified Christ in Holy Week*, The Liturgical Press, Collegeville, Minnesota, 1986.

Walter J. Burghardt SJ, *Preaching – The Art and the Craft*, Paulist Press, New York, 1987.

Daniel Corkery, *A Munster Twilight*, Mercier Press, Cork.

Anthony De Mello, *The Prayer of the Frog*, Gujarat Sahitya Prakash, Anand, India, 1988.

James A. Feehan, *Stories for Preachers*, Mercier Press, Cork and Dublin, 1988.

James F. Finley CSP, *Wake Up and Preach*, Alba House, New York, 1986.

Billy Graham, *Angels – God's Secret Agents*, Hodder and Stoughton, London, 1977.

Richard Harries, *Prayers of Hope*, from Radio 4's *Prayer for the Day*, British Broadcasting Corporation, London, 1975.

A. M. Hunter, *Preaching the New Testament*, S.C.M. Press, London, 1981.

A. M. Hunter, *The Parables, Then and Now*, S.C.M. Press, London, 1982.

Irish Liturgical Commission, *To Proclaim His Word*, I.L.C., Carlow, 1988.

Harold S. Kushner, *When Bad Things Happen to Good People*,Avon

Books, Madison Ave, New York, 1981.

Denis Lane, *Preach the Word*, Evangelical Press, Welwyn, Herts, 1986.

Mark Link SJ, *Illustrated Sunday Homilies*, Tabor Publishing, Valencia, California, 1988.

Jack McArdle SSCC, *It's Really Very Simple – Uncomplicating the Message*, Columba Press, Dublin 1985.

National Conference of Irish Priests, *Being a Priest in Ireland Today*, Dominican Publications, Dublin, 1988.

Christopher Nolan, *Dam-Burst of Dreams*, Weidenfeld & Nicholson Ltd, 1981, Pan Books, 1988.

Christopher Nolan, *Under the Eye of the Clock*, Weidenfield & Nicholson Ltd, 1987, Pan Books, 1988.

Henri Nouwen, *The Wounded Healer*, Doubleday, Garden City, 1972.

Gerald Priestland, *Priestland's Progress*, British Broadcasting Corporation, London.

Karl Rahner, *Renewal of Preaching*, Paulist Press, New York, 1968.

James A Saunders, *God Has a Story Too*, Fortress Press, Philadelphia, 1979.

John Shea, *Stories of Faith*, Thomas More Press, Chicago, 1980.

John Stacey, *Preaching Reassessed*, Epworth Press, London, 1977.

John Stott, *I Believe in Preaching*, Hodder and Stoughton, London, 1982.

John Stott, *The Cross of Christ*, Inter Varsity Press, Leicester, 1986

John V. Taylor, *The Go Between God*, S.C.M. Press, London, 1972.

Leo Tolstoy, *The Power of Darkness*, trs. L & A Maude, Constable, London, 1914.

Simon Tugwell, *New Heaven, New Earth*, Darton, Longman and Todd, London, 1976.

Pol Vonck WF, *Parables, Stories for Retelling*, Gaba Publications, Eldoret, Kenya, 1981.

Robert Waznak, *Sunday after Sunday, Preaching the Homily as Story*, Paulist Press, New York, 1983.

William R. White, *Speaking in Stories*, Augsburg Publishing House, Minneapolis, 1982.

STORIES FOR PREACHERS
James A. Feehan

Part of the challenge facing the preacher today is getting the message across Sunday after Sunday. Only too often he faces a television saturated congregation which seems either unwilling or unable to listen to him. If he doesn't actually hear the click of the switch-off, then one glance at the glazed looks in the pews should convince him that the pulpit may well be losing the battle with the box.

Stories for Preachers is written from a conviction that the massive boredom in our churches today stems from the fact that the average Sunday worshipper is incapable of sustained listening for more than a few minutes. If it can't be said in six to seven minutes it can't be got across at all. The short homily calls for long and painstaking preparation and needs to be illuminated by apt and imaginative illustrations.

Christ taught and preached in stories. His stories were from real life; stories about farmers and fishermen, weddings and wakes, self-righteous humbugs and prodigal sons. The preacher today is faced with the challenge of bringing the reality of Christ to a people bewildered by the fantasies of the media.

Stories for Preachers is an attempt to meet this challenge through the storytelling process. Its aim is to assist the preacher in proclaiming the 'old, old story' and in the process perhaps sow the seeds from which his own creative thoughts will develop.

MY NEW CURATE
Canon P.A. Sheehan

'It is all my own fault. I was too free with my tongue. I said in a moment of bitterness: "What can a Bishop do with a parish priest? He's independent of him." It was not grammatical and it was not respectful. But the bad grammar and the impertinence were carried to his Lordship, and he answered: "What can I do? I can send him a curate who will break his heart in six weeks..." '

My New Curate is one of the most powerful of Canon Sheehan's very popular books. It was acclaimed all over the world as a vivid picture of the relationship between a priest and his flock and it is reprinted here for the benefit of whole generations who did not have the opportunity to read it.

Patrick Augustine Sheehan was born in Mallow, Co. Cork in 1852. He was orphaned when he was ten and became the ward of the Bishop of Cloyne. He was educated at St. Colman's College, Fermoy and Maynooth. He became Parish Priest of Doneraile in 1893 and Canon in 1903. He was dogged by ill-health all of his life and this may have resulted in the intense interior life that made him a great novelist. All of his books were very popular and were translated into several languages.